Improving School Behaviour

Improving School Behaviour

Chris Watkins and Patsy Wagner

P·C·P

Paul Chapman
Publishing Ltd

Paul Chapman Publishing Ltd
A SAGE Publications Company
6 Bonhill Street
London EC2A 4PU

SAGE Publications Inc.
2455 Teller Road
Thousand Oaks, California 91320

SAGE Publications India Pvt Ltd
32, M-Block Market
Greater Kailash-I
New Delhi 110 048

British Cataloguing in Publication Data
A catalogue record for this book is available from the British Library

ISBN 0-7619-6336-7
ISBN 0-7619-6337-5 (pbk)

Library of Congress catalog card number available

Typeset by Anneset, Weston-super-Mare, Somerset
Printed and bound in Great Britain by Athenaeum Press, Gateshead

Dedication:

To all those who have talked out of turn
and, at least once a week,
made unnecessary (non-verbal) noise;
and to Douglas, Etta and Fred,
three great improvers.

Contents

List of figures and tables

Introduction

Welcome to this text. We intend you to find it useful.

As a whole in this book we aim to offer you ideas, arguments and examples which will allow you to see issues of school behaviour in the most constructive way possible, and to think through some appropriate forms of action to follow. Is that what you were expecting? Take a moment, if you will, to unearth any expectations you have as you start this text: not only will this help to activate your reading, but it might also help you gather your skills of handling disappointment! – not everything you might expect will be found herein.

What is in the chapters?

In the first chapter we have to consider how behaviour is explained, since this has a major knock-on effect as to how action is devised. In schools we are surrounded by different forms of explanation, some of them more productive than others. Improving school behaviour can mean improving the explanations. This chapter also brings forward the evidence which supports the 'multi-level' approach we adopt.

Chapter 2 addresses an area which some teachers baulk at – school behaviour. 'It's not the school that behaves, it's the pupils' they say to us. We disagree and consider the way that different schools behave, together with how aspects of the school as an organization influence the patterns of pupil behaviour. Improving school behaviour can involve a range of action at this level, and is generally much more productive than making up reactive school policies.

The classroom is one of the most complex social situations on Earth, and this has to be understood before we can think sensibly about approaches to improvement Chapter 3 distils much research about the many factors which influence classroom behaviour, and leads to a diagnostic framework.

In adopting a multi-level approach we do not ignore the individual, and Chapter 4 offers frameworks and examples for making sense of patterns of behaviour at this level. It also leads into thinking which can help to develop appropriate action, and which links up to other levels of action when needed.

Finally, Chapter 5 focuses on the working relations between staff over matters of behaviour. It contrasts the repetitive relations in a referral system with the productive relations in a consultation system. With some of the frameworks from earlier chapters and on extra focus on process, working relationships can be developed to minimise difficult school behaviour.

Using this book

As the above outline may have indicated, the order of chapters is deliberate. We feel you will get most out of the book by gaining a sense of the important perspective in Chapter 1, before moving into the different levels in Chapters 2, 3 and 4, where school and classroom deliberately come before individual. The evidence for this approach is to be found in Chapter 1. But we recognize that many readers will want to go straight to a chapter which interests them – we do this ourselves as readers. Perhaps the best we can hope for is that you might read this book in a similar way to how A S Byatt describes her reading of a novel – a quick skim to find out the main plot, followed by a more detailed read of the episodes which attract.

We do hope you will use this book, and that you might do more than read it. We hope we have presented ideas and practices which you can adapt into your own practice, and we hope to regularly encourage you to talk about what you have read (and done) with your colleagues. That is the way that change really happens.

Why are we writing this?

We have a 'because of' reason and an 'in order to' reason. We write because of the many occasions when we see matters of behaviour handled in ways which make things worse. A school might formalize a reactive policy which leads to more exclusions; a classroom teacher might 'tighten up discipline' and worsen the learning relationships; another colleague might handle interactions with a particular pupil in such a way that their dignity is eroded rather than enhanced. On all such occasions the outcome is not what anyone really wants. It could be otherwise, even in the busy and crowded place we call school. So we write to put in place some constructive alternatives.

Twelve years ago we wrote a text which had some similar structural features to this book: a multi-level view to create a 'whole-school approach'. Part of our motivation then was to combat the distortion of pastoral care systems into discipline dustbins, and to move beyond the prevalent within-person explanations for difficulties. Those motivations remain, and have been enhanced by our experiences and what we have learned from them over the intervening years.

What is this book based on?

The knowledge base which informs this book comes from the work and thinking we have been involved in for many years. Chris Watkins is a senior lecturer at the University of London Institute of Education, and has run many courses in the area of school behaviour. He has facilitated dozens of school in-service days on the theme, regularly hearing the comment 'that's the best day we've ever had'. Working with teachers at higher degree level on this theme means that he has to be up to date with the international research evidence. Patsy Wagner is an educational psychologist in Kensington and Chelsea who has pioneered a consultation-based approach for education psychology services working with schools, and works closely with teachers and parents in a multi-level way. She is regularly involved in consultations with teachers, and sometimes with parents, on many concerns some of which may include the difficult behaviour of individuals, groups and classes. But for both authors, the theme of behaviour is one strand of our work, which is as it should be. We are sceptical about any job which is completely devoted to behaviour, since it appears to say that this focus is a goal in itself. It is not. We work in this area in order to release people's energies for the real work: effective learning, good tutoring, positive personal-social development, and so on.

Over the years, we have been privileged to work with many colleagues in England, Wales, Scotland and Northern Ireland, as well as Hong Kong and Norway. Our publications have been translated into Spanish and Cantonese. Throughout these experiences, we have learned how to improve the ideas and how we communicate them. We have also learned the limitations of what we offer.

Who says we need to improve?

The life of educators in many 'developed' countries has increasingly become the focus for hostile comment over recent decades. This book is not part of that trend. When we say 'improving school behaviour' we are not criticising you or your school; we are merely setting out the ground – things could be better. As colleagues in school improvement have often remarked, 'You don't have to be ill to get better'. So we feel that nearly every school situation in which we find ourselves could be better, and as a result pupils, teachers and others would feel better about their work, relationships and achievements.

So are things getting worse?

We recognize this question in this introduction because we are often asked it. Perhaps people ask because in Britain the public climate regarding school behaviour is regularly a critical one, made so by the way in which national and local media select and sensationalize their coverage. This process is not new: Pearson (1983) offers a fascinating account of how public fears regarding 'hooliganism' were constructed in Victorian times.

It seems that favourable behaviour does not sell newspapers. Sensationalized reports have a role in amplifying deviance, in heightening public fears and setting off debates about reactions which may not be needed. With regard to crime generally, many people in the United Kingdom believe there is much more crime than there actually is, and with regard to school behaviour, difficulties are distorted. The problem is that people seem to believe such accounts, including journalists in neighbouring countries, one of whom recently stated 'UK teachers are regularly subject to intimidation and assault' (*Cork Examiner*, 1997). Even in USA, where estimates suggest that 135,000 school students each day take a gun to school (cited in Welsh, Greene and Jenkins, 1999), experienced researchers in the area have tracked a number of indicators of school violence over the past 20 years and concluded: 'As was the case 20 years ago, despite public perceptions to the contrary, the current data do not support the claim that there has been a dramatic, overall increase in school-based violence in recent years' (Hyman and Perone, 1998, p. 9). Historical analyses show us that 'pupil riots' were much more common in the early part of the century (Humphries, 1981), and that in England the most extreme act of violence from pupils to teachers – a plan to shoot them at a staff meeting – was planned in 1947 (Adams, 1991).

If we only believed what we see in press coverage we might think that school behaviour is getting worse, but there is not an available database which could provide us with evidence that pupil behaviour is in fact getting worse – or better, for that matter. Sometimes surveys are carried out (and we will analyse these in Chapter 1) but they are based on various reports rather than direct evidence. Nevertheless, numbers of teachers tell us that they feel behaviour is getting worse. That feeling is real and is worthy of concern.

Significant increases in pupil exclusion are with us, but these cannot be taken at face value as a direct reflection of worsening pupil behaviour. Rather they can be seen as a reflection of the reactive approach encouraged by central government policy-making and legislation over a number of years. It also relates to the sudden growth of out-of-school provision such as 'pupil referral units'. As a result there is a more widespread sense that exclusion is an acceptable response. In the process some young people have lost their right to full-time education.

What does feel clear to us is that school practice is not improving in significant or widespread ways. Our schools are subject to increasing demands for particular sorts of performances, and to increasing add-on accountability. This can divert and narrow their attention, away from the very things which contribute to healthy behaviour and effective achievement. When goals and relationships are left unattended, the first signs can be worsening pupil behaviour.

So, overall, we do not find it fruitful to pursue the question 'Are things getting worse?' – rather we offer the following ideas on 'Working together, things can be better'.

1

The picture we create: explanations and levels

In this chapter we set out key ideas for the rest of the book. We start by considering the way in which behaviour difficulties are viewed in school, and how they are explained to self and to others. Common everyday explanations are analysed, and the disempowering effects on teachers are discussed. We then present 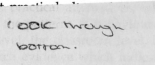 also help colleagues in a school discuss ʻ ᴏᴏᴋ ᴛʰʀᴏᴜɢʜ three important levels: the organizational ʙᴏᴛᴛᴏᴍ . the individual level. We look at the rese that improving school behaviour must me

Identifying difficult behaviour

It is important to start by recognizing that different perspectives on what constitutes difficult behaviour exist in our schools. This is not some simple matter of sloppy subjectivity or relativism: it is a fact of social life. We find that a small proportion of teachers do not like this point: they say that it introduces unnecessary complications and remark 'Why don't we just agree on what behaviours are difficult and what we'll do to deal with them'. Our reply is that we have seen groups of teachers in schools do that time and again, and either end up in conflicts or with little change occurring. The reason is that such agreements paper over real variations, some of which will always exist and can be used profitably for improvement. As we will see in Chapter 2, the dressing up of such agreements as 'school policy' has little positive effect in the majority of circumstances.

The diversity of views on school behaviour which are to be found in, around and across school staffrooms is not something we wish to bemoan. Though we accept that in a few schools there is too little commonality between teachers, this usually betrays some other major difficulty or conflict in the school. Most times the diversity is appropriate, and can be a source of learning. Our view is that it is important for teachers to identify and discuss their different ways of seeing, but not to aim for some unrealistic consensus. It follows that we do not expect progress will follow from us (or anyone else) advocating a single definition for difficult behaviour.

Take any behaviour you like, which you think people would agree was difficult or deviant in a particular situation: you can always think up another situation in which it would not be seen as such. Whether a particular act is regarded as deviant varies in a range of ways, including those which follow.

- *According to place.* In school Mary's singing may be viewed differently in the art room, in the music room, in the head's room. What Mary does outside the school gates may be perceived differently from the same action inside. Across different schools, what a pupil may do acceptably in one may be completely unacceptable in another.
- *According to audience.* Nigel's critical comment about a teacher while discussing his behaviour with his tutor will probably be seen differently from the same comment made while his tutor is teaching the form. When an inspector becomes an additional audience in the classroom, both pupils and teachers change their behaviour. When visitors tour a school, an additional or accentuated set of rules for what is acceptable is often activated: 'best behaviour'.
- *According to the actor.* Linda has a reputation for disrupting lessons: her behaviours may be seen and responded to differently from the same behaviour by classmates who do not have such a reputation. A Year 7 pupil with unexplained absences may be perceived differently from a Year 11 pupil. Denise's direct physical aggression may be seen as more deviant than Denis's. A pupil arguing with teacher may be seen in various ways, perhaps depending on whether the pupil is a child of a lawyer or of a bricklayer. John's behaviour in the corridor is viewed as 'over boisterous', but similar behaviour from Joel who is Black British is perceived differently.
- *According to the observer.* Mrs Williams has seen John pushing in the dinner queue three times before: she sees things differently from Mrs Jones who has not. Mr Frederick has a real concern about bullying: his reaction to events differs from that of his colleagues.

- *According to who is seen as harmed.* Andrew taking a ruler from his friend in the same year is viewed quite differently from him taking a ruler from a pupil in the earlier years. Ann jostles people in the crowded corridor: this is viewed as 'playful' towards her apparent friends but not towards Maria in her wheelchair.
- *According to time.* Steve's shortage of equipment for lessons is seen in a different light when the school has a 'purge' on equipment: similarly for 'drives' on homework or attendance or uniform. Hassan's exuberance is perceived differently on Monday morning than it is on Friday afternoon. The perception of Julie's talking at the beginning of the lesson is different from that of her talking at the end.

So, identifying difficult behaviour is not a matter of simple definition. Instead our attention is drawn to variations in contexts and variations in explanations.

Explaining difficult behaviour

Typical everyday explanations in school

When attempting to improve school behaviour we soon come face to face with the explanations for difficult behaviour which circulate in a school, their variety and any prevalent explanations or trends. These explanations can have a significant effect on improvement attempts – for good or ill. Teachers' explanations reflect, in part, real evidence about patterns of difficulty: they also reflect a range of distortions or partial perspectives. We will examine five broad explanations which we have encountered in our experience of schools, and which are sometimes referred to in the literature. We use the broad everyday phrases and offer a range of examples:

- 'They're that sort of person'
- 'They're not very bright'
- 'It's just a tiny minority'
- 'It's their age'
- 'This is a difficult neighbourhood'.

As we discuss each in turn, you might think of examples which you hear in school, and also consider the impact of their use.

'They're that sort of person'
Examples such as 'Jeremy is an aggressive boy' serve to show how this way of talking attempts to package everything about difficult behaviour into some feature of the person. It is classic 'within-person' thinking. 'He's a special needs kid', someone remarked, as if the analysis should end there. We are not saying that this sort of talk is always making neg-

ative evaluations of the pupil in questions: one memorable one was 'Ah but you have to understand that this pupil has Bohemian parents', and the speaker was not referring to a new refugee group but was wanting to explain the behaviour difficulties by recourse to family attitudes. Of course there are broad trends which link family attitudes to performance at school, but these cannot be simply invoked in an individual example. In a similar way, the use of prevalent stereotypes about single parents or separated and reconstituted families ignores the great range of ways in which families respond to and cope with such conditions, and so does not offer an adequate explanation in the individual case. Examples which contradict the 'family background' explanations are regularly found in school, but such evidence is often resisted:

> Some teachers expressed astonishment when pupils were exception-
> ally resistant to teacher influence despite an apparently supportive
> home background. They were equally surprised if model pupils were
> inadvertently revealed to live under adverse home circumstances.
> Faced with a rebellious or uncooperative pupil, teachers were often
> prepared to assume that there be something wrong at home even if no
> evidence was immediately available.
>
> (Chessum, 1980, p. 123)

A similar simplification is that which assumes that a pupil's behaviour at school mirrors behaviour at home. Interesting light is thrown by the findings which showed that when teachers and parents completed similar rating scales for the same children there was comparatively little overlap between the 'disorders' perceived by both groups (Graham and Rutter, 1970). So, even if teachers were identifying a similar overall percentage to that of surveys, and attributing family explanations, they may be identifying a different group of children from that identified by parents! The behaviour which pupils display in school is not a simple reflection of their behaviour elsewhere, including at home (see, for example, Rutter, 1985a). In the case of those pupils where the conventional wisdom is that their behaviour varies less than most according to situational cues, i.e. pupils categorized as having severe learning difficulties, just under half are reported to have challenging behaviours both at school and at home, and the particular behaviours displayed and seen as challenging are different in each context (Cromby *et al.*, 1994).

Nor is behaviour at secondary school a simple continuation of behaviour at primary school. Secondary schools with poor pupil behaviour are not simply those which receive a high proportion of pupils with a record of behaviour problems at primary school (Rutter *et al.*, 1979). 'There was only a weak relationship between behaviour at primary and secondary schools' (Mortimore, 1980, p. 5).

The 'they're that sort of person' view seems to be an attempt at explanation, but at the same time seems to reflect some powerlessness in the teacher's attempt to understand – 'they're just like that' (and I cannot say any more). Nevertheless the use of this explanation can have action implications: for example, if the pupil's behaviour is disturbing, then this explanation may be used to justify a referral to whoever is supposed to deal with 'that sort of person'. Those case-based professionals who sometimes practise with an individualistic view of people are then engaged, and in this process their ability to 'fix' certain individual problems is mistakenly overestimated, sowing the seeds for teachers' subsequent disappointment at their offering. Within-child explanations are much more a feature of reports by headteachers and educational psychologists (Table 1.1), than they are of interviews with parents (Galloway, Armstrong and Tomlinson, 1994).

Table 1.1 Explanations of heads, psychologists and parents

Principal causal or contributory factors referred to	Reports by head teachers (n = 26)	Reports by educational psychologists (n = 22)	Information from one or both parents (27 children)
Child (e.g. low ability, behaviour etc.)	18	17	10
Family	8	4	5
School	0	0	14

Source: Galloway, Armstrong and Tomlinson (1994).

'They're not very bright'

This teacher explanation could be seen as a variant of the previous one, but it deserves special attention since it brings to the fore beliefs which are particular to school contexts and to pupil attainment. Judgements about pupil 'ability' have an extra significance in the school context and are closely connected with the way school is organized: in some schools beliefs about fixed ability circulate regularly, in others less so. When related to difficult behaviour, we can hear examples or variations of these: 'Some of these disruptive kids try to hide the fact that they can't get on with the work by creating diversions' or ' They get frustrated with the work and then start to mess around'. A moment's thought clarifies that this explanation embodies significant beliefs and assumptions on the part of the speaker regarding classrooms, curriculum and school. These assumptions often imply what can change and what cannot. If they lead to a more detailed examination of how to modify the curriculum or the classroom context in ways which engage such students, all well and good. In contrast, to accept such an explanation in a fixed form would imply that pupils of particular 'abilities' will be disruptive. Such an alternative is unacceptable. The explanation 'if they're not very bright, there's nothing we can do about it' is a recipe for a passive response rather than an improving response, because it embodies a notion of innate or fixed abilities rather than one of learning potential. A way forward is more likely to come from considering how pupils of all current attainment levels can be engaged in learning.

'It's just a tiny minority'

This explanation recognizes that there may be a pattern in the numbers of pupils involved, but locates the cause in a very small number. Many social systems contain beliefs that their dangerous miscreants are small in number but have a disproportional effect because of contagion effects: one rotten apple can spoil the whole barrel, etc.

It can be useful to reflect on what 'tiny' is. Evidence from in-school surveys has indicated up to 15 per cent of the pupils on roll are mentioned by name in connection with disruptive incidents monitored across two terms (Lawrence, Steed and Young, 1977). Hardly a tiny minority. Nor even the 'hard core', because although only 1 per cent of students were mentioned in incidents from both of the weeks monitored, these were only a small proportion of the incidents which staff viewed as serious, numbers of which involved large groups of pupils. So a picture emerged of more general disruption with a varying group of pupils involved, making it more profitable to examine the patterns of pupil roles (see Chapter 3) than to locate *the* cause in one or two individuals.

Another feature of the 'it's a tiny minority' explanation is the implication that 'tiny minorities' are distinctly different from 'us' (who, of course, are part of the majority): they are portrayed as obeying very different rules (or no rules) and are so different (from us) that it is unlikely we would be able to understand them. Thus, the accentuation of differences is achieved, and if there were any real differences they are greatly exaggerated. A good antidote to this trend is to help teachers remember their histories – some of them were skilled disrupters – or to have them simulate a classroom and have the roles emerge. Disruptive pupils are not an inherently different group but the pressure to portray them that way seems strong.

The action implication of the 'it's only a tiny minority' explanation is to identify them ('early' if possible) and extract them. 'If we get rid of the troublemakers, everything will be all right'. But that is no solution in the long run. Unless such separation is strictly temporary, the facility for separating pupils will tend to 'silt up'. It also works once only: when it is full, schools continue to want to refer to the provision they have become accustomed to, and meanwhile in the classroom, new members have emerged to fill the deviant roles of those who were removed. 'Pressures build up within (the schools) for more provision, which is then created – and soon fills up, and so on. In this way many problems of behaviour are apparently coped with, more are created, fewer are solved' (Rabinowitz, 1981, p. 78).

This is the sort of partial thinking behind the provision of 'pupil referral units' in England and Wales in the 1990s. There are always more procedures for processing pupils into these units than there are for processing them out, so the provision fills up, contrary to the official protestations that this was meant to be short-term provision. It also grows: a survey we completed in 1995 (unpublished) found some units with over 200 pupils on roll. The vast majority are told to attend for less than 15 hours per week. It seems like the growth of part-time schooling in our cities for those who are excluded from school. Yet the pressures of league tables and standardization are significant: just as in the 1970s, many policy-makers bend to the trend. Young, Steed and Lawrence (1980) found that where heads and teachers form a majority on local education authority (LEA) 'disruption' working parties, the setting up of units was more likely: where they formed a minority a broader approach was adopted, including some critical consideration of the curriculum, improving in-service training and increasing support and advice.

The authors of this book were both involved at times in the management of similar, though school-based, provision in the 1970s. At that time of considerable growth in on-site and off-site provision, major difficulties were identified for the aims and rationale, referral and clientele, methods and achievements of such provision (Mortimore *et al.*, 1983). Although we believed that units could provide important temporary support, they were often not successful in altering patterns of disruptive behaviour, mainly because their practice so firmly locates the cause with the pupil, rather than the interaction between pupil and the context to which only a minority returned. For those who were reintegrated, 'problem behaviour re-appeared in over 60 per cent' (Daines, 1981, p. 107). In the new pressures of the 1990s, schools in greater numbers are considering on-site units. No doubt they will once more collect pupils with a great diversity of need, and young staff with considerable dedication, but they will not address the wider issues which lead to their creation: curriculum, organization and teaching-learning processes. What may also be worrying is that they risk creating divisiveness in a school community and feelings of resentment among a group of pupils (Tattum, 1982).

'It's their age'
This explanation is prevalent in everyday talk. The very term 'adolescence' seems to necessarily conjure up images of difficulty for some

people. Folk theories such as 'young people have to challenge authority' abound, and show us how certain psychological theories derived in the clinic have been popularized. Occasionally a biological determinism is added, 'it's their hormones': we have even witnessed a meeting where a deputy head attempted to explain the downturn in exam results by recourse to hormones. Stereotypical views of adolescents as moody or unpredictable or having identity problems or being excessively influenced by their peers are evoked – as though these were realistic views of all adolescents or (to the extent that they are valid) as though they applied to adolescents alone, or to disaffected adolescents more than others.

The age in question is nowadays disputed by some commentators. Those publicized examples of primary-age children who are associated with disruption have led some people to argue that 'the age' is coming down. But the major pattern remains: the age group with which most difficulties are related is the later years of secondary school. It is only a shorthand form of communication which describes this pattern as a product of pupils' age: the explanation does not lie in any absolute quality of age (i.e. of being 15 years old) but rather in the position which the pupils have reached in their school career (i.e. one or two years before the officially permitted leaving point). The pattern reflects pupils' increasing awareness of the impending transition to non-school life, and the lack of perceived connection of their school life to their future. The appropriateness of curriculum, teaching approaches and teacher–pupil relations are all brought into focus, as are organizational aspects. School continues to be one of the most rigidly age-segregated organizations in our society, yet we do not make creative use of this aspect for engaging adolescents and their wish to be recognized as young adults. It is perhaps no surprise that some studies conclude 'disruptive behaviors were limited to rules and conventions related to the social-organizational aspects of school life (which is) not correlated with a rejection of rules related to moral issues (e.g. harm, rights, fairness)'. (Geiger and Turiel, 1983, p. 682). Progression in status and responsibility of pupils as they progress through school can be minimal. As a result, many are able to exercise only minimal responsibility (sometimes only the self-restraint which teachers wish) at school, which is in marked contrast to their responsibilities at home and in part-time employment (Bird *et al.*, 1980). Schools which actively engage students in the life of the organization and engage older students in the helping of younger students generally have better behaviour.

'This is a difficult neighbourhood'
Our clearest example of this was in a school serving a small leafy county town. It was not based on any objective measure of disadvantage in the

local community: rather it was a world-view built up in the school – 'we are the crusaders here and the heathens are all around us'. The missionary connotations of early education come spilling out in negative views of the natives. In different ways the talk in some schools can portray them as embattled against the outside world. But again the facts do not confirm that neighbourhood is a simple 'cause': schools in similar or the same neighbourhoods can be associated with differing pupil behaviours (delinquency, attendance, behaviour, achievement), as school differences research in England and Wales has shown from the start (Power *et al.*, 1967; Reynolds and Murgatroyd, 1977a; Rutter *et al.*, 1979). A recent sophisticated analysis of school and community data for 11 schools in an area confirmed that 'neighbourhood' is no simple explanation: 'We conclude that simplistic assumptions that "bad" communities typically produce "bad" children or "bad" schools are unwarranted' (Welsh, Greene and Jenkins, 1999, p. 73).

The action which is implied or sought by users of this explanation seems limited. In part that shows why it can be so destructive, to attribute cause to something well beyond teachers' reach. But perhaps also it is because some larger issues are implicated. It is the case that the neighbourhoods which schools serve are polarized by socio-economic status – increasingly so. The UK is a society with considerable social divisions and a powerful sense of hierarchy – more so following the increase in inequalities during the 1990s, assisted by the education rhetoric of 'choice' and policy of 'open enrolment' to secondary schools. Educational success through schools is distributed differentially along lines of social class, so there are important patterns to address, and although we cannot view socio-economic class as a single 'variable', we cannot ignore it just because it is not neat to analyse. Much of the difficult behaviour in some schools is associated with older working-class pupils. The structural inequalities of class and 'race' are not easily changed by the efforts of educators, and general approaches to school improvement are insufficient to reduce this overall pattern (Mortimore and Whitty, 1997), but we know that schools in difficult circumstances can succeed despite the odds (National Commission on Education, 1996), thanks to exceptional commitment of staff. Overall the education system needs targeted support in disadvantaged areas to overcome the corrosive effects of increasing inequalities. With that and with well-tuned approaches to improving behaviour in each school, we believe that unequal patterns can be reduced. In the mean time, neighbourhood offers no explanation for individual patterns of behaviour. Pupils from all parts of the socio-economic spectrum have remarkably similar views on school, teachers and the curriculum (Inner London Education Authority, 1984).

Effects of 'inside the person' and 'outside the walls' thinking

We have seen that these five broad sorts of explanations present a partial or an exaggerated picture, and they do not serve us well if we are seeking to explain. But there is another effect which is more disturbing: the repeated use of these explanations has a disempowering effect on teachers. This is a point which teachers themselves are not slow to recognize. One group of teachers in a working session were asked to report what they felt the effects were: they replied 'lowers morale' and 'may keep us stuck'. On another occasion with the large staff of a school, the underlying process was described to them as 'teachers colluding in their own disempowerment' – an unusual and perhaps challenging phrase, but one which they asked to be repeated since it had really struck a chord.

It is interesting to wonder, briefly, why this state of affairs exists. In part, it reflects two processes which are repeated in many contexts, those of individualizing difficulties and externalizing difficulties. Individualizing occurs partly because our language encourages it: the sentence construction of subject–verb–object leads us into 'Jeremy created a riot' and a consequent focus on Jeremy. It seems more difficult, forced even, to say 'In the context of the classroom, some of the behaviour was seen as riotous, and Jeremy played a significant role in it' (although, as we shall see, this construction will lead to more options for improvement). Our language may not have been helped by dominant and popularized versions of psychology: Gergen (1991, p. 13) has argued that 'the vocabulary of human deficit has undergone enormous expansion within the present century', and we often find people in school using such vocabulary in sloppy ways. Externalizing difficulties is not peculiar to schools. In many other organizations which are not learning well, there is a tendency to say 'the enemy is out there' (Senge, 1990). It happens most in a climate of blame, and can be seen as an understandable human response. But some organizations, some schools, do it more than others. The negative effects show it is a poor trade-off: by painting themselves out of the picture, teachers can feel worse and things can get worse; by diverting the reasoning for difficulties away from the school, they throw away the power to change, and good chances for learning and for improving the state of affairs.

If we are to move onward it will entail the use of explanations which are not so simplified and which paint the teacher and the school back into the picture. This cannot be done if it seems to merely shift a dynamic of blame: we used to blame the children, now we blame the teachers. But it can be done: there is nothing fixed about explanations. Evidence from other countries makes the point: 'The first question many Danish teachers ask themselves about the pupil who is difficult is "What have I done or failed to do that could account for this?" The term generally applied to such children's behaviour is "tiredness of schooling" ' (Steed, 1983). Teachers' judgements in different countries reflect the fact that what is seen as problematic can vary: Langfeldt (1992) showed that teachers in Germany perceive aggressive behaviour as more problematic than do their counterparts in South Korea, and non-conformist behaviour as less problematic.

Different schools are also characterized by the predominance of different explanations: some specialize in family background attributions, others in the folk theories regarding age. Here the important point is that they relate to success or not. Those schools which see themselves as part of the picture in patterns of difficulty use exclusion less, because they believe the problem of disruptive behaviour to be within their power to resolve (Maxwell, 1987). In some schools teachers share information to help student learning, they seek help widely to solve problems and increasingly come to believe that student learning is possible with even the most difficult students: in other schools teachers may swap stories about a child's errant behaviour, focus on behaviour as though disconnected from learning and see punishment as the solution to problems (Rosenholtz, 1989). The former schools are more successful: they do not blame, either pupils, their families or themselves, but they actively seek solutions.

Different contexts within school are linked with different patterns. Many of the 'explanations' of pupils which bounce around the staffroom with the morning coffee serve as an important release from the stress of teaching – they do not necessarily surface in front of another audience on another occasion, nor do they necessarily influence those teachers' behaviour towards pupils in the lessons which follow the coffee. Further, the situation in which a teacher is talking about pupil behaviour that has thwarted their goals is often one in which their emotions have become understandably engaged. It is not in itself a difficulty that teachers display emotion, but in this situation emotions may lead us to focus on our own perspective, see less of the overall picture, and use more limited explanations.

At the level of the individual teacher, too, those with richer descriptions of long-term problem-prevention or remediation strategies are also the ones who are rated as highly effective at dealing with problem students, and express more confidence in their ability to elicit significant improvement (Brophy and McCaslin, 1992). Whereas those teachers who believe that the causes of difficulty lie solely outside the school are also those who predominantly use internal systems for 'referral' (Evans, 1999).

Think about conversations in your school when pupil
behaviour is being discussed. They could be in meetings,
in general conversation, in case conferences, and so on.
What sorts of explanations are being used (implicitly or
explicitly)?
Are they predominantly any of the above explanations?
Do you think there may be particular purposes behind the use of
these explanations? And hoped for actions?
Do you see any longer-term effects which follow from the
overuse of particular explanations?

Improving explanations

So what is the way forward in terms of explanations? We all need to have
an explanation in order to be able to cope and to carry on with school
life, so it is not a matter of merely giving them up, but substituting more
constructive ones which recognize wider connections and patterns. In this
way teachers' explanations can become more professional and more
reflexive, that is they include themselves in the picture. One of the hallmarks of the professional is that they can take a perspective on their
work, and on the social pressures which influence it.

There is, perhaps, reason for optimism to be gathered from other data.
If we switch attention from the 'causes' or 'origins' of difficult behaviour,
to the means of improvement, teachers place themselves more centrally
in the picture. Miller (1995) interviewed 24 teachers and extracted the
attributions they made to parents, pupils and themselves, both for the
origins and for the improvement of difficult behaviour (Table 1.2).

Steps towards improvement can apply these findings to the everyday
talk between colleagues in a school. Following the recognition that some
forms of explanation keep us stuck in our thinking and offer no routes
to generating solutions to problems, it is possible to make explicit
agreements not to overuse forms of explanation such as those discussed
above. One enjoyable method we have used to get this process started
uses an old television game show strategy from the Yes/No interlude in
Michael Miles's *Take Your Pick*: colleagues are told that at any time in discussions of behaviour they may respond to overuse of within-person or

Table 1.2 Number of different causes attributed by teachers in respect of the
origin and improvement of difficult behaviours

	Parent	Pupil	Teacher
Responsibility for origin	15	21	10
Responsibility for improvement	3	13	20

Source: Miller (1995).

externalizing talk by gonging the speaker out with an imaginary gong. Despite fearful predictions, our experience is that this leads to a large amount of mirth and an increase in more reflexive conversations.

An associated step is to promote talk about improvement rather than about cause. This brings the teacher back into a professionally balanced perspective, and is a key dynamic in making improvements at any level: individual, classroom or school.

Other steps move on from interpersonal talk, and some of these are not so amenable to change in the short term, since they focus on the practices of the school and the ways of thinking which are embedded in those practices. As we have said above, use of pupil referral units displays an individualized form of explanation: as we shall see in the next chapter, use of internal referral systems can be counterproductive if based on individualized ('inside the person') and externalising ('outside the walls') explanations. But these processes can be improved or altered if, first, a shared understanding is reached that their current practice benefits no one in the longer term. This is a necessary first step: without a shared understanding that the practice has become 'stuck', any subgroup of staff are unlikely to obtain agreement to change it on their own.

Changing the discourse

It is now necessary to identify what sort of explanations may move us on towards options for change, in contrast with those which can get us stuck.

There are three main elements in talking about difficult behaviour which will improve the discourse, and these are developed in the remainder of this chapter, with practical application throughout the rest of the book. They are:

- looking for patterns and looking for exceptions
- identifying cycles of productive and non-productive sorts
- seeing behaviour in context, with its associated idea of levels of analysis.

The use of these styles of talk has an important effect. Teachers have known for many years 'don't focus on the person, focus on the incident' – this is an element in many interventions which use assertiveness or conflict resolution. But a further step is to move from a focus on incident to a focus on pattern, trying to identify the various occasions when a difficulty occurs, the sequence of events, and so on. This has an associated effect of bringing the context, (including the school and the teacher) into the picture in appropriate ways. It often leads one step further into strategies for change where a principle of dialogue is present, improving the communication about the various pictures which people have created.

Look out for this trend in improving discourse about behaviour:

person → incident → pattern → dialogue.

Contexts and situations

One of the most important statements for developing an improved under-standing of behaviour is 'B = f(P.S)', written by a key social psychologist, Kurt Lewin, over 50 years ago (Lewin, 1946). It means: behaviour is a function of person and situation.

You can doubtless think up many examples in accordance with this principle, especially in relation to your own behaviour, because we have the tendency to explain our own behaviour in terms of the situations we are in. But we do that much less for others: we explain their behaviour by recourse to something about them, some trait or disposition. Perhaps this 'fundamental attribution error' (Jones and Nisbett, 1972; Ross, 1977) helps explain the persistence of the 'they're that sort of person' view. But the facts do not support it: studies of people's behaviour demonstrate that the extent to which they are consistent across situations is very small – 'Correlations between scores on personality scales designed to measure a given trait and behaviour in any particular situations presumed to tap that trait rarely exceed the .20 to .30 range' (Ross and Nisbett, 1991, p. 95). The classic studies of social psychology have demonstrated the power of the situation in influencing human behaviour: no such power-ful studies exist to demonstrate the power of stable attributes in an indi-vidual. A person may show remarkable consistency of a particular behaviour in a particular situation, but from there on the individual pic-ture varies markedly, while the situation remains powerful.

The principle also applies to pupils and difficult behaviour: 'findings indicated that children's disruptive school behaviors are not reflective of stable, long-term traits possessed by individuals . . . Additionally, there is indication that the students' disruptive behavior did not generalise to all social situations' (Geiger and Turiel, 1983, p. 682). And it is unusual to find a pupil who is disruptive in all situations of school life (Hargreaves, 1980).

You will see throughout the rest of this book that we use this princi-ple in a number of ways: to understand the classroom situation and what it does to teachers and to pupils, to understand which situations in a par-ticular school are associated with difficulties and to identify the situa-tions in which problematic individual behaviour occurs. At this point we need to clarify why we have organized and ordered our considerations in the way we have.

A multi-level view of behaviour

As we shift our way of thinking to patterns, and take seriously the power of contexts, we see that difficult behaviour in school can present patterns of both large and small types, encompassing few or many situations. We have come to display this in the style of Figure 1.1.

Of course Figure 1.1, like all diagrams, is a simplification of a complex picture: the school as an organization is comprised of multiple classroom situations, and other situations too – they are not portrayed; the classroom is composed of many interacting individuals, and so on.

Nevertheless, conceptual and practical benefits follow:

1 These three levels are not merely a product of this sort of analysis: they are each contexts which have a directly observable influence on behaviour. As students and staff cross the boundary which marks the school, their behaviour changes – each morning and each evening. Throughout each day, as they cross the boundary which marks out a particular classroom, or the different activities within a classroom, their behaviour changes again. So the contexts are very real.
2 We can identify and separate different levels of analysis. The elements which are associated with difficult patterns of behaviour at the organizational level are of a different type and scale than those at the individual level. We need the appropriate concepts and language for the appropriate level, and to make clear the level of phenomenon we are talking about and seek our explanations at that level. Sometimes our attention properly shifts from one level to a wider one if, and only if, we have evidence that wider patterns really exist. In that sense there may be connections which are made by data.

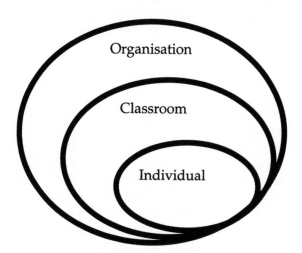

Figure 1.1 Three levels of patterns in school behaviour

3 We can direct our efforts sensibly in the short term, by using the level of analysis and concepts appropriate to the focus in hand. For example, when focusing on an individual it is useful to temporarily 'park' our thoughts about organizational patterns: when making sense of Diana's behaviour it is not so helpful to use wider explanations such as 'schools create that sort of behaviour' – they divert our attention. Another example, when making sense of the patterns of behaviour of a particular year group, it will be helpful to consider aspects of that year's standing and history in the school organization, but not so helpful to invoke an explanation such as 'they're a lazy lot' (an individual within-the-person level of hypothesis).

4 In the long term we need to understand and work on all three levels: that is what research demonstrates is most effective, and it may be most appropriate to call a 'whole-school approach' something which works on all three levels. Therefore on one of those occasions when a particular incident has led (some) staff to call for a whole-school response, we can know that the first priority is to manage the incident and its effects, and then later to consider any wider patterns of which it may be a part.

5 Placing one element inside another recognizes that each has in turn its own context, which could have significant effects on the patterns of behaviour in each element. We could have included wider contexts such as community and society. But we could read too much into that. Assumptions about hierarchies can enter unwittingly so, just because school is 'larger' than classrooms, some people read this to be saying that the organizational level is more powerful. We do not encourage this reading: it could blind us to the fact that each level can make itself fairly impervious to direct influence attempts from the 'higher' level. If we had included the government in the context outside the school we would be saying that its influence on school patterns should not be assumed in some simple hierarchical way (we will say elsewhere why we think any impact UK governments may have had in the 1980s and 1990s has been negative, but in the main it has been ineffectual, as is usually the case for distant influences on behaviour in loosely coupled systems).

6 Each level has a different motivational process and different approach to change. Individuals are motivated to affiliate, achieve and influence, and these forces can be harnessed for pro-social behaviour. A classroom community is motivated to function well, create a constructive climate and a feeling of success in its members. A school generally seeks to survive as an organization, make a difference to young people's lives and to the community it serves. Although there may be connecting themes there are also different improvement processes.

Improvement at all three levels

There is one study of improving school behaviour which stands out from the field. Generally, the theme is not well served with comprehensive research studies on approaches and interventions: much of the research adopts a partial perspective (sometimes the author's favourite theory), and the literature is fragmented. The exception is the work of Denise and Gary Gottfredson (Gottfredson, Gottfredson and Hybl, 1993).

The Gottfredsons carried out a three-year eight-school study of improvement, in a group of schools which were by no means easy: they were much more punitive than most and had adopted the US practice of keeping students behind a year – almost half of them in one case. The principle of three levels of analysis was clear from the start:

> Research implies that misbehavior in schools has determinants at three levels:
> (a) some individuals are more likely than others to misbehave
> (b) some teachers are more likely than others to produce higher levels of misconduct in their classroom by their management and-organization practices
> (c) some schools more often than others fail to control student behavior.
> Behavior change programs that reduce risk for misbehavior at all three of these levels are most likely to be effective.
>
> (ibid., p. 182)

Schools worked on a range of strategies, and improved significantly on student reports of classroom order and classroom organization, whereas a group of comparison schools did not improve.

At the whole-school level, schools reviewed their various practices and policies, and made better provision for systematically rewarding desired student behaviour: they also introduced a behaviour monitoring system on computer, which additionally was used to generate letters to parents to encourage them in reinforcing desirable behaviour.

> ... these changes were not sufficient to reduce student misconduct and rebellious behavior, Those schools that *in addition* significantly reduced the amount of punishment and changed the school climate in the direction of respectful, supportive, and fair treatment of students experienced beneficial student outcomes. This suggests that simply adding a cosmetic system of positive reinforcement onto a punitive system is not productive.
> ... Schools that implemented only the school-level components did not experience positive change. Most misbehavior can probably be traced to classroom- and individual-level sources that the school-level components did not alter. Although the school-level components prob-

ably helped to set the context for alterations in these more proximate domains, they were unable to stand on their own.

(ibid., p. 209)

At the classroom level, a guide to classroom organization and management was offered (Emmer *et al.*, 1989), but a most important method was used. Rather than the guide being 'adopted' or 'implemented', teachers worked in improvement teams, selecting and experimenting with the support of their peers. In this way the technological components of the programme (computers and systems) were supported by staff development activities and structures. Teachers were also given feedback on progress, in terms of results from a measure of classroom environment. The conclusion was:

> Classroom-level changes . . . appeared effective for modifying student behavior. We are unable to disentangle the effects of preventive classroom management changes from changes that targeted troublesome students . . . but it is clear that a combination of these approaches was effective for producing improvements both in the orderliness of the classroom environment and in teacher and student reports of student behavior.
>
> (ibid., p. 213)

The method was important. This study had clarified the different extents to which the various schools implemented the innovations – an unusual step in such studies (Gottfredson, Gottfredson and Skroban, 1998). In one case, the computer was overemphasized, in another there were leadership difficulties, in some the positive emphasis was ignored. Having recorded this, the researchers were able to conclude: 'High implementation schools differed from medium implementation schools in higher use of rewards for group behaviour, higher intervention to prevent misbehaviour, and greater team effectiveness' (Gottfredson, Gottfredson and Hybl, 1993, p. 199, Table 3)

Team effectiveness was a key component, much more significant than the 'training' of individual teachers:

> The classrooms of those teachers who participated as members of a school improvement team . . . had more positive outcomes. These teachers received more training in the program components than the other teachers in the school, but the study results suggest that it was the team participation rather than the additional training that led to the improved outcomes. Teachers in the schools whose teams were ineffective also received more training, but their classes did not improve.
>
> (ibid., p. 209)

The key messages from this important study are:

- Adopt a three-level approach of reviewing and developing practice, not a simple bolt-on.
- Engage and support teacher teams in creating improvement, not an individual training approach.
- Monitor and feedback progress on important measures such as the classroom environment.

Principles of improving school behaviour

First check your assumptions for improvement. Do they reflect any of these:

- developing methods for gaining compliance?
- developing methods for maintaining classrooms in some teacher-centred form?
- developing methods for learning about behaviour and thereby improving our schools and the learning in them?

This book will help with the third position in the above list. Not only is this the most likely to have a positive impact, but we view the other options as anti-educational or unethical.

The second step is to map the current situation in the school, attempting to adopt a multi-level view. This will prevent you wasting time addressing phantom problems, but instead will enable you to obtain a picture of the real pattern of difficulties in the school.

A good map of the difficulties leads easily into what we will call a 'diagnosis'. We are not here wishing to call up any connotations of doctors or medical models of understanding difficulty: rather we want to use the term 'diagnosis' to suggest an overall understanding of a school or classroom or individual, including any patterns of difficulty which may be associated with it.

Good diagnosis leads to good intervention, and most good interventions demonstrate the same level of uniqueness as the situations they address. It is likely that a team of insiders in any school, supported through appropriate frameworks for thinking and action, will be best placed to devise and implement the intervention.

Review is a key to learning, and needs to be planned in so that the effectiveness of the intervention can be evaluated. On many occasions, teachers do not give themselves credit for successful interventions which have contributed to improving a pattern of difficulty. Review leads to celebration.

Check your assumptions

Map the difficulties

Devise the intervention

Review the impact

What do these principles mean we will not do?

- Overestimate the patterns of difficulty and what it will take to change them.
- Adopt ready-made packages without a detailed diagnosis of their appropriacy.
- Adopt somebody else's favourite solution to our unique situation.

Being proactive

At all levels in the chapters which follow, we will consider the evidence which convinces us that reactive approaches are counterproductive – at school, classroom and individual levels. By a reactive approach we mean any approach where the staff's action is defined in response to a pupil's misdemeanour. The opposite is a proactive approach where staff anticipate and analyse and limit patterns of difficulty before they arise – again, at school, classroom and individual levels. We have found over the 1990s that reactiveness is endemic in many of the hidden assumptions about improving school behaviour, and is explicitly sustained by many sources. But it does not work in the long term. We have also found that this is superficially recognized in some schools, but we say superficial because underneath the school is not learning. Peter Senge (1990), in an analysis which is not derived from schools or difficult behaviour, states that one of the ways in which organizations do not learn is through the illusion of taking charge: 'Sometimes what people claim is "proactiveness" is reactiveness in disguise. True proactiveness comes from seeing how we contribute to our own problems' (Senge, 1990, p. 21).

The challenge for us in intending to improve school behaviour includes the challenge of finding a way of addressing real patterns of difficulty in such a way that simple corrosive processes of blaming are avoided in favour of a more comprehensive understanding of a range of contributions, including our own.

2

How does your school behave?

In this chapter we consider how to make sense of the school's effect on patterns of behaviour and how interventions at this level contribute to improving school behaviour. Research discussed in Chapter 1 shows that the whole-school level provides an important context to interventions at other levels, and must be a part of improvement efforts. At the same time it is not enough on its own.

We start by selecting and justifying some of the ideas we will need in order to understand the school's effect, and in order to talk about our contribution at this level. Then it becomes possible to identify which important aspects need to be addressed in our own school. At the same time we indicate why so many of the approaches generally proposed have so little effect. Having identified the difficulties which occur, we have to consider the range of interventions that might be possible: is it some sort of policy? An assertive discipline package? A reward drive? A social programme? The range of alternatives seems considerable and we offer considerations which help to narrow the choice, and principles for effective work at this level.

School effects on behaviour

Time was when people discussed difficult behaviour in schools without referring to anything about the school. This still happens from time to time, but in the main new understandings are available which allow the school's contribution to difficulties to be discussed. Some understandings have been founded in research and others have not, but they are now part of our everyday vocabulary. To use an official example, the school in the North of England which attracted massive media attention surrounding difficult behaviour was analysed in its inspection report (HMI, 1997) using terms like 'relationships deteriorating rapidly', 'confrontational stance', 'insufficient in-service training and monitoring' and 'The school . . . is in a weak position to carry out a thorough analysis'. The point here is that the report uses ideas about key aspects of the school: its interpersonal climate, the support and learning systems, and the organization's ability to analyse. These are a part of the professional language which we can bring to bear, whether or not our newspapers and politicians do so.

When discussing the school's contribution to patterns of difficulty, there are those voices who cry 'that's it – blame the teachers', but they are letting emotions get the better of their analysis. It is an understandable response in a climate of public blame such as that which has been generated and employed by politicians and their agencies in the UK successively during the 1980s and 1990s, but when it comes to improving the behaviour in a particular school we have to put those influences to one side, as much as we can, in order to focus on the proactive strategies we can develop together. Here the language used must not trigger feelings of blame in individual teachers, but must focus on the style and processes of the organization itself. As we have seen in the previous chapter, it is a curious defence which seems to say 'these patterns are nothing to do with us', but such explanations which leave us out of the picture are mostly offered when we feel impotent. The challenge is to find the most productive way of discussing the school's contribution, to paint ourselves back into the picture we have inadvertently painted ourselves out of and to find how it can be improved.

Schools do make a difference

It is said that up to the 1970s the view was held that schools were unlikely to have major effects in the face of home background and social class.

This view was supposedly based on sociological studies of the period which actually measured nothing of the school process, so were able to attribute educational difference to larger societal variables. However, since the 1970s we have seen how schools are associated with differences which cannot be explained simply by recourse to pupils or neighbourhood. Such findings substantiate well the view which many teachers and parents have always held – that different schools have different overall effects on a variety of outcomes for their pupils, not merely the narrow range which are currently represented in 'school performance tables'.

In the 1960s studies of schools in the East End of London showed that schools with comparable intakes in the same area were associated with markedly different rates of delinquency among their pupils (Power *et al.*, 1967). On another indicator, studies of secondary schools in Sheffield (Galloway *et al.*, 1982) demonstrated large and consistent differences in the number of pupils excluded or suspended on disciplinary grounds. In South Wales (Reynolds and Murgatroyd, 1977a; 1977b), levels of truancy were shown to differ consistently across schools in the same area with similar intakes, and these differences were maintained over some years. So the school was shown to be making a difference in areas of concern such as behaviour. Other studies (Minuchin *et al.*, 1969; see also Minuchin and Shapiro, 1983) separated out the effects of school from the effects of home, and demonstrated that school has a significant impact on wider matters: pupils' sense of self, images of life possibilities and conceptions of how a social system beyond the family functions.

While demonstrations that schools make an independent difference were important for the efficacy of educators, a continued search for school differences *in contrast* to home differences would have been fruitless since it may oversimplify a complex situation. Both home and school can be powerful influences and, ideally, both act as positive influences in an additive way, with positive school effects having to work in concert with positive family/home effects. However, school is not a sufficiently powerful social agency to alter the larger patterns of social disadvantage in society, although with well-planned intervention it can prevent social disadvantage becoming educational disadvantage as well (Mortimore and Whitty, 1997). Crucially, in individual cases where family or life experiences and influences are negative for a young person's development, school can provide a protective environment.

Different schools make different differences

Even at the earliest times of studying school differences, it was clear that schools did not make a single uniform difference. On all sorts of dimensions it was clear that different schools were associated with different patterns of impact. One study (Cannan, 1970) suggested that even the style of delinquency and its age of onset varied across comparable schools: one was associated with more petty theft while in another pupils specialized in 'taking and driving away'. More broadly, a study which contributed to the growth of the field now called school effectiveness (Rutter at al., 1979) showed significant differences between 12 London schools on a range of behaviours. In some schools the incidence of difficult behaviour was five times greater than others. The study chose the notion of school ethos to explain differences between schools: this may have been an appropriate explanation, but the ethos of the 12 schools had not been measured throughout the study, so it was a *post hoc* explanation which did not build on many earlier studies of ethos or climate.

In professional discussions the idea of the school effect is now generally accepted. However, it does not always follow that professionals know what their role might be in doing something about the school effect, especially in their own organization. Teachers often show signs of disempowerment when such matters are raised for discussion. This is often a reflection of the language which has been used to describe the school effect: if we cast it in terms of a monolithic and depersonalized effect, everyone will feel disempowered. So here again the challenge is to go into further detail about how such effects happen, and in the process paint ourselves back into the picture.

What is it about the school that makes the difference?

In many of the early studies of school differences, the mechanisms and processes through which schools make a difference were not spelled out in detail. In that sense these studies were 'black box' studies, which showed different 'outputs' for similar 'inputs', but could not say much about what had occurred in between. To find more detail, we need to turn to other sources; studies which focus on school behaviour and relate it to school-level phenomena, and to studies of schools as organizations which include some focus on behaviour.

In selecting ideas for the first half of this chapter, we have sought ideas and strategies which are:

• manageable and malleable
• based in research, hopefully intervention research
• likely to generate interventions which have a long-lasting effect.

We do not claim that we have completely achieved this – the lure of the quick fix is very strong and clear in the literature on school behaviour – but we have come as close as we can.

A helpful approach was adopted by Wayson *et al.* (1982). They wanted to investigate the characteristics of schools reputed to have good discipline. Through professional networks and contacts with nearly 1,000 people, more than 1,000 schools were identified and surveyed in order to describe the activities in which they engaged to get 'good discipline'. The results of their investigation, the characteristics of well-disciplined schools, included the following list:

1 These schools did many things that have been done by good schools and good educators for a long time (i.e. no new tricks, no quick fixes).
2 These schools create a whole-school environment that is conducive to good discipline rather than adopting isolated practices to deal with discipline problems.
3 Most teachers viewed the school as a place where staff and students come to work and to experience the success of doing something well.
4 These schools are student oriented.
5 These schools focused on causes of discipline problems rather than symptoms.
6 Programmes in these schools emphasized positive behaviours and used preventive measures rather than punitive actions to improve discipline.
7 These schools adapted practices to meet their own identified needs and to reflect their own styles of operation.
8 The headteacher plays a key role in making these schools what they are.
9 The programmes in these schools often result, either through happy coincidence or through deliberate design, from the teamwork of a capable head and some other staff member who has the personal leadership qualities that complement those of the head.
10 The staff of these schools believe in their school and in what its students can do; and they expend unusual amounts of energy to make that belief come true.
11 Teachers in these schools handle all or most of the routine discipline problems themselves.
12 The majority of these schools have developed stronger-than-average ties with parents and with community agencies.
13 These schools were open to critical review and evaluation from a wide variety of schools and community sources.

As you read this list, you will probably find yourself reacting and questioning: for example, 'what sort of critical review?' or 'what do they mean by student oriented?' That is exactly what this list is very useful for: to stimulate discussion about what people think a 'well-disciplined' school is like. An approach here is to use it for school self-evaluation: reproduce it on a sheet, and ask colleagues to indicate the three characteristics which in their view are most clearly present in the school, and the three characteristics which they see as most in need of development. This then becomes the starter for a group discussion and further analysis. In our experience teachers often identify items 11 and 6 as most in need of development, but patterns and discussion particular to individual schools are also stimulated and probably more important than trends across schools.

As well as providing a tool for initial evaluation, this list generates discussion about people's conceptions of well-behaved schools. In our view the important thing about the picture which is created is that it is a healthy proactive organization which does not adopt piecemeal or reactive stances, and an open organization which pays attention to its social processes. There are implications for the style of leadership needed to achieve this at all levels.

Machine or social system?

At this point a crucial issue in our understanding of improving school behaviour is highlighted: it seems that well-behaved schools are effective social systems, and to become more like them we need to consider how to improve various social processes. But very many of the interventions which are suggested for improving school behaviour treat the school as a machine, and ask what add-on can we think of which will fix this? The distinction between social system and machine is important when viewing the school as an organization, since the approaches to change are likely to reflect one or other of these stances. Staff in a particular school will not necessarily recognize this difference, or its importance, in our experience. Indeed, those who have triggered themselves to seek a quick fix will not want to consider it. However, the leaders of an improvement effort will need to recognize it. They will need to be aware that many on the outside of school – politicians, various advisers and trainers – will appear to sell quick fix add-ons where it seems that one size fits all. The reality of school improvement (Stoll and Fink, 1996; Stoll and Myers, 1998) has shown us that improvement does not come this way. Instead we need to have the ideas to understand and then move to identify the particular needs in a particular school.

We now consider four major ideas which might help you identify important issues that underlie the patterns of behaviour in your school.

A   The school as proactive or reactive

As we said at the end of the last chapter, being proactive is crucial at any level: organization, classroom or individual. Let us clarify the term we are using through a distinction: being proactive involves anticipating potential difficulties, thinking ahead rather than waiting for them to arise. In contrast, being reactive means only responding to current problems, and planning a response once they have arisen. In the real-life day-to-day management of schools and classrooms it is not possible to be purely proactive, but the balance between these two is crucial. For improvement attempts to be successful and to have continued impact in the long term, they must be predominantly proactive. The evidence for this statement comes from a range of sources which tell us that reactive approaches can make matters worse. Let us now consider some of that evidence.

The phenomenon of excluding pupils from school has attracted attention in the UK over recent years. It is not possible to view this as a simple reflection of deterioration in pupil behaviour (Watkins, 1998): we see it as more a reflection of competition between schools in the context of 'league tables', increasing provision of 'pupil referral units', and a less responsive curriculum which creates an atmosphere more prepared to consider exclusion. Within that broad picture, different schools display markedly different patterns: 'Some [secondary] schools were far too ready to exclude pupils; others did so with extreme reluctance' (Office for Standards in Education, 1996, p. 7).

These different patterns reflect a reactive or proactive approach to thinking about difficult behaviour and the practices which follow. There has been evidence for some time that higher rates of suspension are to be found in schools where senior staff tend to have less confidence in their own power to tackle the problem of disruptive behaviour (Maxwell, 1987). If key people believe the problem of disruptive behaviour to be within the power of schools to resolve, then the practices and outcomes are more positive. If not, then systems and practices become distorted and ineffective. For example, the pastoral system in a secondary school becomes inappropriately turned into a reactive discipline system, with worsening results:

> In high excluding schools (but not exclusively) year heads and heads of house worked hard but were often overwhelmed by numbers of pupils referred to them for indiscipline by classroom teachers. Frequently such referrals short-circuited established systems and merely reflected the unwillingness of some staff to deal with problems at source. As a result, such problems often escalated and, although pastoral heads spent much time with difficult pupils, often that time achieved little other than to register concern and pass sentence. In the schools which provided good pastoral support, the key factor was that the importance of tutoring was recognised.
>
> (Office for Standards in Education, 1996, p. 19)

Similar distortion can occur in the primary school, where the role of a deputy head can become reactive through class teachers treating him or her as the person to whom naughty children are regularly sent. If the frequency of such interactions is low, then the balance might remain productive, especially if staff consultations are held as a result.

Reactive approaches may also be identified in the area of school policy on behaviour, a growth area in UK schools during the 1990s. Here the distinction between proactive and reactive is very marked. Reactive approaches to policy include those which we call 'the tariff approach', in which school staff somehow agree and codify a set of responses to particular student misdemeanours. The very form of this approach – 'If they (the pupils) do X, then we (the teachers) will do Y' – is a good definition of being reactive. If this is the main or only response to difficult behaviour, it is likely to make matters worse.

In the UK, it has now reached the stage where official inspections of schools identify reactive policies as a contributory factor in the rising number of exclusions:

> In some cases an increase in numbers of exclusions can be attributed to the application of new stratified codes of conduct in which exclusion is a 'fixed penalty' on a sliding scale: whereas in the past, for example, incidents of fighting were dealt with by pastoral staff as arbitrators and conciliators, many recently adopted behaviour codes stipulate temporary exclusion as the punishment for fighting.
>
> (Office for Standards in Education, 1998, p. 66)

A headteacher telephoned one day to discuss the scheme which had recently been adopted in the school: he expressed some concerns about the patterns which were starting to emerge, and finished with 'I think there must be something wrong, because I've just suspended a mild-mannered girl, basically for not taking her coat off, all because we had reached that stage in our new system'. What became clear was that the school had adopted a tariff approach in which a staged set of responses to pupil misbehaviour were agreed, and that repeated misdemeanours led to movement through these stages, culminating in exclusion. The key issue was that movement through the stages was automatic, dependent only on what stages had been reached previously, and involving no alternative routes or professional judgement. These features created a pattern of increasing exclusion.

In a primary school in Hampshire a teacher had adopted a similar approach with a staged set of responses in her classroom. The patterns of behaviour were not improving: indeed, the classroom atmosphere was getting worse. An experienced inspector worked with the teacher and held discussions with the pupils. Their view was that this new system needed to be tested: it seemed to them to be an automatic set of rules, and if this was the case they would see the teacher as not caring about them.

So reactive approaches to policy can be counterproductive, but in the UK, schools are now required to have some sort of policy on behaviour. This is a matter of regret, since there is a tendency to view 'policy' as a set of statements. This encourages an erroneous view of the school as a policy-driven machine, and can discourage attention being directed to the important social and learning processes of the school. It may also encourage a 'one size fits all' approach, where statements apply to all events and professional interpretation and care are downgraded.

Most important, there is evidence that school policies of the sort which focus on agreeing, understanding, and consistently enforcing rules and sanctions have no effect on improving student behaviour. A two-year study of such intervention in the Australian state of Victoria (Hart, Wearing and Conn, 1995) gathered data from 4,072 teachers in 86 primary, secondary and special schools. The results showed that, on average, teachers believed things had improved slightly (this is a feature of many school interventions), but that no difference was made to the mean levels of student misbehaviour. 'These findings also suggest that teachers may mislead themselves about the actual effectiveness of programmes, resulting in them stopping successful programmes, or continuing with unsuccessful ones' (Hart, Wearing and Conn, 1995, p. 36). Further, in a context of increasing exclusion, the causal models which were generated from the data showed that there was no direct relationship between student misbehaviour and student suspension rates. 'These findings strongly suggest that student suspension rates should not be used to indicate the degree of misbehaviour in schools' (ibid., p. 43).

Overall, reactive approaches can encourage rule-laden inflexibility, and this has been related to various forms of disaffection. Reynolds (1976) studied patterns of truancy in nine South Wales secondary schools and related it to features of the teacher–pupil relations. He concluded that consistent and ongoing differences between the schools could best be explained by noting that in some schools pupils and teachers struck a truce over the application of some rules, whereas in other schools pupils and teachers refused a truce. Thus there was a remarkable lack of conflict in the social life and interpersonal relations in some of the schools.

> A crucial factor in determining a favourable overall response by the pupils to most of their schools lies in the degree to which both staff and pupils have reached an unofficial series of arrangements, or truces, which lay down the boundaries beyond which the participants in the schools will not carry their conflict.
>
> (Reynolds, 1976, p. 132)

Thus truces may be struck over a range of issues which are not directly related to learning, for example, some aspects of dress, chewing gum, and so on. Then 'lessons are no longer the focus of conflict between teacher and taught' (ibid., p. 133) In the schools where no truce existed, an anti-school subculture had developed by the beginning of the third year. Teachers in these schools attempted to ensure their control through increased coercion: pupils' commitment to school reduced, and teachers consequently had lower expectations of the pupils.

So what could a proactive policy look like?

Now that we have seen the possible difficulty in adopting a reactive approach, what might a proactive approach to a school behaviour policy look like? The set of contrasts offered in Table 2.1 will start to build some new possibilities.

By developing a proactive policy, a school displays how it considers behaviour and how it intends to improve it. 'An effective behaviour

Table 2.1 Features of proactive and reactive behaviour policies

Proactive		Reactive
A set of principles which guide action	vs	A set of rules
Principles which underlie any rules are clarified	vs	Procedures and enforcement of rules are tightened up
A stimulus to learn	vs	A statement to make public
Appreciates what is currently helpful and anticipates future difficulty	vs	Focuses on what is not working and reacts to difficulty
Reviews any current rules and their effects	vs	Institutes new rules
Builds coherence, harmonization while recognizing variation	vs	Seeks consistency, uniformity
Outlines how to improve: • school facilities • curriculum focus on behaviour • classrooms and their management • staff systems for learning/development • engaging pupils' views	vs	Outlines what teachers are to do if pupils do X
Phrased to engage everyone	vs	Phrased to apply to pupils
Promotes the handling of difficulties close to where they occur, e.g. in the classroom	vs	Promotes referral (e.g. to deputy head, head of year) and potential escalation
Problem-solving is based on conceptual analysis and understanding	vs	Problem-solving is based on trial and error
Attempts to understand 'causes' close at hand	vs	Attempts to implement 'cures' from any source
Uses teamwork to address difficulty	vs	Uses isolated individuals with separated responsibilities
Problem-solving is organization-wide and problem centred	vs	Problem-solving is compartmentalized and hierarchical
Total school approach, covers all three levels: organization, classroom, individual	vs	Fragmented strategies, covers the administrative level
Promotes and reflects the school goals, other school policies and culture	vs	Stands alone (promotes and reflects a fragmented culture)
Specifies its own review mechanisms	vs	Does not consider a review

policy encapsulates the school's *thinking* about behaviour: its application shows the school's determination to *affect* school behaviour rather than accept it as a given' (Office for Standards in Education, 1996, p. 17).

The last word on policy should be this broad reminder: when a school makes a policy, it makes an image of itself and its vision of the future (after Tomlinson, 1986). The image of themselves which some schools make in their policies on behaviour is a Victorian prison: in such cases the future is non-existent. By contrast, other schools can create an image of themselves as social learning communities: they embrace the future and help young people to do the same.

A related area which also reflects the unwitting adoption of a machine perspective on the school occurs when people claim that improving school behaviour is about 'increasing consistency'. Consistency is a weasel word: different people use it in different ways and they often do not spot the differences. In one person's usage it means something bordering on uniformity, whereas for another person it means a complex coherence. The term 'coherence' has been preferred by analysts in this field for some time, and is clearly distinct from uniformity.

> One characteristic of a climate favourable to the working through of appropriate responses to disaffected behaviour was what, for want of a better term we identify as staff coherence. In contrast to other schools ... some schools were grappling with their institutional problems in coherent and consistent fashions. There was no single model of staff coherence, nor a simple explanation of how it functioned in any one school ... Coherence should not however be confused with uniformity. Many personal styles and differentiated skills can be exhibited within a coherent staff team.
>
> (Bird *et al.*, 1980, p. 123)

Calls for consistency can sometimes be counterproductive to staff coherence. One evening in a south London boys' school, a self-selected working party of staff were discussing how some of the difficulties in the school could be remedied by greater consistency among the staff. They were gently but professionally challenged to clarify who held this view, how they had derived it, and so on, until one colleague said 'I've just realized – we as a group might be using this in an attempt to get the group who aren't here to be more like us'. Well spotted – the intensity of the micro-politics between staff on these occasions can be considerable, and mostly they go without being discussed.

Consistency in itself is not a valuable commodity – things could be consistently bad. The sort of rationales which suggest 'Pupils need more consistency – they can't be expected to change from one situation to the next' is not only inaccurate, it is likely to be damaging. Pupils' responses to teachers' different strategies show complex patterns in which most of the variation is explained by the interaction of the person and the situation (O'Hagan and Edmunds, 1982) – this is exactly as it should be for young people developing a complex interpersonal repertoire: for healthy development, they need to learn how best to respond differently in different situations.

'Codes' in schools

Some schools have developed 'school codes'. When these are effective, they are not long lists of rules: these are likely to elicit from some pupils the very behaviour which teachers do not want (self-respecting adolescents love to test boundaries). They are a clear and defensible set of principles for the school whose reasons should be obvious: their source is rational authority, not power. They apply to and have been developed by all groups in the school, who thus wish to see them operate in practice. Consequently they are not phrased at the level of simple behaviours.

Here is the start of an example from a primary school in Staffordshire. It connects rights and responsibilities in a very constructive way:

1 We have the right to an education and to learn according to our ability.
  We have the responsibility not to ridicule others for the way in which they learn, or to disturb the learning of others.
2 We have the right to be treated with respect by all people irrespective of age, gender, colour or status.
  We have the responsibility to respect all others within our community.
3 We have the right to feel safe in and around the school.
  We have the responsibility to ensure the safety of all pupils by behaving in a reasonable manner in and around the school.

In the context of this discussion of 'consistency', it needs to be said that a code such as this does not remove the need for interpretation – indeed, it is in the interpretation of principles to daily incidents that pupils and teachers learn. So codes do not suddenly generate uniformity in a complex organization such as a school, but they contribute to harmonization in a principle-led community.

How proactive is your school?   low └──┼──┴──┘ high
In your view, what developments would improve this rating?

B The school as a collaborative organization

The degree to which staff in a school collaborate with each other has an important impact on the patterns of behaviour at the organizational level. This issue has already been hinted at in relation to the collaboration needed if proactive approaches are to be developed, but its influence extends much wider than that, into many aspects of the social fabric of the school. The degree of collaboration between teachers in a school is associated with the view they have of teaching, the way they solve problems and their response to difficulty.

Specifically, in schools with higher degrees of collaboration, when teachers share information about a particular student, it is usually for the purpose of finding ways to help the student learn more effectively. This contrasts with what is found in schools with higher degrees of isolation: here sharing information about students usually takes the form of swapping stories about a child's errant behaviour or sympathizing with one another. Another important difference relates to what teachers do when they have a particular difficult problem with a student. Teachers in collaborative schools seek help more widely, seek to identify causes and then to solve problems, whereas for teachers in isolated schools problems invariably means behaviour problems, and punishment is seen as the solution (Rosenholtz, 1989). In more collaborative schools colleagues more readily assist each other, and they do so without pejorative implication that someone has failed to control their class and to do it on their own.

Collaboration is also a strong predictor of student achievement gains. In 78 primary schools which Rosenholtz studied, gains in reading and maths were measured for one cohort of students from 8 to 10 years. A regression analysis controlled for school socio-economic status, school size, teacher experience, teachers' verbal ability, and pupil–teacher ratio: it showed greater gains in collaborative schools.

Collaboration among teachers is also associated with positive relations between pupils. Metz (1986) observed that schools whose teachers cooperated with one another were also characterized by co-operation among students and interracial harmony. Stevens and Slavin (1995) demonstrated that the use of co-operation as an overarching philosophy to change primary school and classroom organization and teaching-learning processes is related to significantly higher achievement and better social relations. This applied to all students: disabled students were more accepted socially by their able-bodied peers, and gifted students had significantly higher achievement than gifted students in less co-operative contexts.

If pupil learning is greater, so too is teacher learning. In schools where collaboration between heads and staff and among staff was the norm, teachers felt they continued to learn about their profession throughout their careers. Conversely, when collaboration was not the norm, teachers tended to believe that they had learned all they need to know about teaching within the first few years after entering the profession (Rosenholtz, 1989).

Teacher collaboration for teacher learning thus becomes an important focus. Teaching can be an isolating profession, more so than almost any other profession. In that sense teachers have been described as 'psychologically alone in crowded environments'. As a result it has often been the case that teachers' classroom practice was 'privatized' – the classroom door closed, and detailed discussion of teaching and learning was rare. In such a setting, teacher learning was limited. But teaching does not begin and end in the classroom. At a minimum, a teacher's experiences with other staff members, as well as with the school's leaders and organizational structure, will cause smiles or frustration. At maximum, these interactions can have a profound effect on the impact that a teacher has on his or her students.

The development of a school-based professional community is nowadays seen as crucial in offering support and motivation to teachers as they work to overcome the tight resources, isolation, time constraints and other obstacles they commonly encounter in today's schools (Kruse, Louis and Bryk, 1995). In schools where professional community is strong, teachers work together more effectively, and put more effort into creating and sustaining opportunities for student learning. Such a development requires structural support through:

- time for teachers to meet and talk
- physical proximity between teachers
- interdependent teaching roles
- communication structures
- teacher empowerment and school autonomy.

It also needs some more human and social resources, such as:

- openness to improvement
- trust and respect
- skills of communication and facilitation
- supportive leadership
- socializing new teachers into the school.

But that's starting to move into our next section. Before we do . . .

> Stop and consider your school as a collaborative organization.
> How would you rate your school? low |___|___|___| high
> What are the strengths of your school, which areas are underdeveloped?
> In your view, how could this rating be improved?

C   The school as a community

Different schools operate to a greater or lesser extent as a community, and nowadays it is easier to make features of this explicit. Bryk and Driscoll (1988) have analysed what a communal organization means in practice. Schools which operate in this fashion:

1 Have developed collegial relations among adults.
2 Promote a 'diffuse' teacher role, which brings teachers into frequent contact with other staff and with students in settings other than the classroom.
3 Attend to the needs of students for affiliation.
4 'Provide a rich spectrum of adult roles [that] can have positive effects on the ways both students and teachers view their work. Adults engage students personally and challenge them to engage in the life of the school' (Bryk and Driscoll, 1988, p. 3).

In their study of 340 secondary schools in Chicago, Bryk, Lee and Smith (1990) showed how schools vary in their degree of communal organization, and how this had an important impact on everything which is important in school. Schools that scored high on an index of communal organization showed higher teacher efficacy and satisfaction, higher staff morale, higher teacher enjoyment of work and lower teacher absenteeism. Students in such schools were more interested in academic achievements, were absent from school less often and were more orderly. Their achievement was higher in the only achievement outcome variable considered – mathematics (Bryk, Lee and Holland, 1993). These findings say something crucial about the way schools are organized: a personal-communal model is more effective than a rational-bureaucratic model (Lee, Bryk and Smith, 1993).

The need to build a sense of community in school is important for its own sake, for engagement and for achievement of the pro-social goals of schooling. But for the particular purposes of this book it is also important, since a strong sense of communal organization is related to less difficult behaviour. When we say a 'strong' sense, we do not mean a dominating or controlling sense of community, nor a guilt-inducing sense: we mean a sense of membership, purposefulness and coherence.

The need to consider community-building in our schools, and the practices to achieve it, are discussed by Thomas Sergiovanni (1994). The basic issue is to shift the focus away from schools as organizations based on contracts and rewards to schools as communities bound by moral commitment, trust and a sense of purpose. 'Community can help teachers and students be transformed from a collection of "Is" to a collective "we", thus providing them with a unique and enduring sense of identity, belonging, and place' (Sergiovanni, 1994, p. xiii).

In broad terms, the three areas of membership, purposefulness and coherence become the principles for a varied range of actions. Attention is paid to becoming a new member of the community, to being an active member of the community (pupils are crew, not passengers) and to including all members of the community so that staff pupils and parents feel trust and respect. Purposefulness is engendered by having a principal goal focus such as helping pupils focus their minds towards learning well, and valuing purposeful activity which meets this principle (e.g. pupil as knowledge-worker). Coherence is enhanced by staying true to the principal purpose, and avoiding the many diversionary invitations which are created or we create. The implications for organizing school and its priorities are many.

Within this theme, we can also focus on the forms of relationships which characterize a community, as distinct from a formal organization. A discussion instrument on the teacher–pupil aspects of such relationships is included.

Teacher–pupil aspects of community relationships

This instrument seeks to highlight features of teacher–pupil relationships in a school, and the extent to which they could be characterized as those of a community.

For each item, please mark on the scale where you feel the overall picture of your school is, between the two poles which are described.

Through the process of responding to this instrument, you may have unearthed ideas and issues which you want to talk over with colleagues. You may also have identified areas of relationship which you consider need improving.

For other purposes, you may wish to make a summary rating of your view at this time. In this case, for each of the six items, convert your scale marks to points as follows:

$$| \quad | \quad | \quad | \quad | \quad |$$

$$2 \quad 1 \quad 0 \;-1 \;-2$$

Total these points across the six items. Theoretically, the total rating could lie between +12 and –12. Scores towards the positive indicate the prevalence of seeing teacher–pupil relations in community terms.

Affective
Teachers' relationships with students are quite warm and engaging

_|_|_|_|_|_|_

Affective neutrality
Teachers' relationships with students are like those of professional to client

Collective orientation
Teachers encourage collaborative learning and support between students

_|_|_|_|_|_|_

Self-orientation
Teachers encourage an individual orientation on the part of students

Particularism
Teachers take into account the unique features of a disciplinary incident

_|_|_|_|_|_|_

Universalism
Discipline incidents are dealt with according to predetermined protocols

Ascription
Teachers value students for being whoever they are, regardless of how well they do

_|_|_|_|_|_|_

Achievement
Teachers value students for their co-operation and achievement

Diffuseness
Teachers believe 'You need to know students well to teach them well'

_|_|_|_|_|_|_

Specificity
Teachers believe that they can enact their roles well with little tailoring to individuals

Substantive
Teachers demonstrate care for students as a core value

_|_|_|_|_|_|_

Instrumental
Teachers demonstrate care for students in order to get better results

Scores towards the negative indicate the prevalence of seeing teacher–pupil relations as part of a formal organization.

Check out whether the school scores significantly different on any of the six dimensions.

Westheimer and Kahne (1993) argue that two essential components can be found lacking in community-building attempts: the first is to provide teachers with experiences which familiarize them with the nature and benefits of strong communities. The second is to equip teachers with the pedagogical techniques to foster and sustain school communities. Teachers, they argue, not only require opportunities for interaction, to build a sense of connectedness and purpose, they also need the support to change classroom practices. Their own curriculum project developed five principles:

- moving from students' experience to theory
- engaging students in common projects
- breaking norms to create opportunities for new relationships
- motivating students within the context of community
- encouraging reflection and respecting dissent.

Stop and consider your school as a community, or communal form of organization.
How would you rate your school? low |___|___|___| high
Which aspects of the school as a community have you highlighted for yourself?
In your view, what developments would improve this rating?

D   The school's approach to learning

The previous two sections have brushed against another dimension which is increasingly seen as crucial to the functioning of a school. The issue of teachers' learning with each other has already been highlighted, and now we consider the school's overall approach to learning, including pupils' learning.

A study which brought this dimension to the fore was carried out as a survey of 52 secondary schools in Victoria, Australia (Cohen and Thomas, 1984). The inquiry was designed to analyse the relationship between frequency of misbehaviours and severity of punishment. The findings were cast as suggesting four disciplinary climates (Table 2.2):

- *Controlled* (low misbehaviour, high severity of punishment). In this category, independent schools predominated: they had a strict atmosphere, authoritarian rules which were spelt out in detail, and a concern with external appearances. Punishments were seldom meted out, perhaps because the whole weight of history seemed to stand behind them.
- *Conflictual* (high misbehaviour, high severity of punishment). Here state schools predominated: they were characterized by an atmosphere of constant tension.
- *Libertarian* (high misbehaviour, low severity of punishment). In these schools there was a *laissez-faire* approach bordering on apathy, combined with a lack of self-direction and lack of concern for others.
- *Autonomous* (low misbehaviour, low severity of punishment). This is clearly the combination to seek. The schools focused on engendering self-discipline; they only had rules which seemed sensible, they

Table 2.2 Four disciplinary climates

| | | Extent of misbehaviour | |
		High	Low
Severity of	High	Conflictual	Controlled
punishment	Low	Libertarian	Autonomous

showed interest and concern for pupil development, and there was active pupil involvement in the learning process.

So, again, promoting pupil autonomy in learning is not just a good in itself, it also turns out to be associated with less difficult behaviour. An additional use of these findings is to indicate the different priorities for improvement towards learner autonomy which might apply for different starting climates. For example:

- The controlled school might need to enhance student self-control in the learning process.
- The conflictual school may need to increase the shared sense of value and purpose in learning.
- The libertarian school may need to develop greater direction in learning and collaboration with others.

If student learning is on the agenda for improving school behaviour, then it follows that everything which influences it also has to be considered: curriculum, pedagogy, grouping practices and so on. All too often school practice in these areas provides the very conditions for worsening behaviour, and all too often the impact of national policies plays a hand. For example, on curriculum, in England, Wales and Northern Ireland, since the introduction of the three subject-based National Curricula we have seen a renewed emphasis on pupils' test performance. Since the advent of league tables and school inspections we have seen an increasingly fearful undercurrent in many schools which is in turn associated with a more standardized attitude to curriculum 'delivery' and a less responsive attitude to pupil experience. At the broad level this has impacted on the general culture of our schools as places for young people to develop. We are told that standards are rising and that schools will be offered annual tests because these have been shown to motivate pupils and enhance performance, but that is a spurious and circular argument. We are increasingly in a situation where performance pressures beget performance pressures and, although the regular use of standard testing may contribute to some increases in performance, there is no evidence that it increases motivation for a wide range of pupils. It may have a stimulating effect for those learners who already show a performance orientation, the mark-hungry children who do it to please, but there is evidence that general pressure does not help pupils at large (Chaplain, 1996; Clarke, 1996). So we are in a state where schools seem to be asked to improve at cramming a curriculum which many teachers feel is not open to meaningful negotiation or review. Would it be any surprise if such a state of affairs was associated with worsened patterns of behaviour, brought about by low teacher morale, and significant groups of pupils who feel fewer experiences of achievement and have their dignity eroded?

On the theme of pedagogy, a very teacher-centred set of assumptions abounds in current talk about teaching, especially that which emanates from government advisers and initiatives. In the face of this, it becomes necessary to remember what decades of research have demonstrated about the need to shift focus from teaching to learning, and to be explicit about the differences between politicians' conceptions and professionals' conceptions of pedagogy (Watkins and Mortimore, 1999).

The next chapter will focus on the detail of classrooms, so here we are mainly concerned with the whole-school messages about pedagogy, and their effects on patterns of behaviour. In one of their illuminating studies monitoring disruptive incidents, Lawrence, Steed and Young (1981; 1989) present the following data from a study of an 11–18 co-educational school. In one week's monitoring, the following number of incidents in classrooms occurred while the type of teaching was as shown:

Whole class	30
Group work	3
Individual work	17
Whole-class and individual work	2
Other	4
Total	56

At first sight this would seem to be striking evidence for the connection between difficult behaviour and particular teaching methods. We consider this would be a likely plausible conclusion. However, there is some possibility that the large number of disruptive incidents during whole-class teaching merely reflects the possibility that whole-class teaching was used a great deal in that school that week, in which case, we could not directly conclude that disruptiveness was related to teaching methods. Nevertheless, this data would certainly suggest that it could be profitable to investigate a possible connection between methods of teaching and classroom management. A similar finding from classes of 10-year-olds found that diversionary behaviour ranging from daydreaming to disruption was more common during individual work and less common in small group and whole-class settings (Silverstein, 1979).

On grouping practices, it is now 30 years since David Hargreaves's (1967) study showed how practices of streaming led to messages of devaluing and to disaffected behaviour on the part of lower streams. Lawrence, Steed and Young (1977) monitored disruptive incidents for two separate weeks in a 14–18 urban boys' school, and showed the following pattern for number of disruptive incidents across 'ability' bands:

	Year 4	*Year 5*
Band 1	5	6
Band 2	11	19
Band 3	34	25

This pattern closely resembled that shown by noting the number of boys named in such incidents:

	Year 4	Year 5
Band 1	9	7
Band 2	5	20
Band 3	25	21

More recently, Taylor (1993) demonstrated that the dynamics of devaluing and disaffection were alive and well in a Leicestershire school. Despite the evidence which shows that ability grouping is related to poor behaviour, and the fact that there is no evidence to support the idea that ability grouping improves results, many schools have responded to current pressures by introducing more setting, banding or streaming.

The paradox is that evidence on school performance does not justify the practices which schools have been adopting, and that those which focus on learning and learner autonomy do well in such terms. Recent evidence on UK secondary schools (Gray *et al.*, 1999) suggests that improving schools have gone through three approaches in the last decade. First, they have adopted new tactics to maximize their showing in the performance tables (enter more pupils, mentor the borderlines etc.). Second, they have adopted internal strategies to improve their schools (giving more responsibility to pupils, building improvement strategies in particular departments, integrating pastoral and academic responsibilities). Third, the small group of the highest improving schools has shifted beyond these two into an area which builds its capacity to improve, through an overarching focus on learning. This third focus is also the one which is related to positive behaviour.

Returning to the theme of schools which promote pupil autonomy in learning, they may also be schools which promote the pupil voice in other community matters, including the solutions to difficult behaviour. A colleague in the north-east of England, who as a headteacher was concerned to reduce graffiti in the school, passed control of the £20,000 environment budget to a committee with a majority of pupils. The graffiti reduced quickly. Schools which are keen to hear the pupils' view on their school are likely to promote a climate in which less difficulty occurs. As Garner (1992) points out, the mechanisms to hear the view of pupils who have been disruptive can be very important: contrary to common assumption, they may have constructive views about school to share.

> Stop and consider your school as promoting learner autonomy.
> How would you rate your school? low ☐☐☐☐ high
> In your view, what developments would improve this rating?

What could work in my school?

As we start to consider action at the school level, two cautions are in order. First the act of asking 'what shall we *do*?' could throw us back into an over-instrumental quick-fix stance, instead of taking on the message of this chapter. Second, the approach to creating change could hold unexamined assumptions. We find teachers readily distinguish the three following approaches to generating change in the current climate: they each have parallels in approaches to changing behaviour.

1 *Problem-solving*. This approach seeks to identify problems, analyse causes, analyse solutions, and develop action plans. It can work well, but if overused there is a danger of exhaustion.
2 *Appreciative inquiry*. This approach starts with a crucial element which we omit at our peril: it is to appreciate the best of what currently is. From finding out what is working well, we can not only do more of it, we can also develop better visions of how things might be, and create dialogue to advance it (Hammond, 1996). More of this approach is needed in UK schools currently.
3 *Ensuring compliance*. In this approach, the first step is to decide what is right, then to promulgate these single solutions, set up a system to regulate and inspect, and punish in public deviants and delinquents. This is the dominant mode from various sources currently, both on behaviour and other matters. Its long-term effects are divisive and demoralizing.

We hope that the first part of this chapter has contributed to some of that crucial re-visioning which appreciative inquiry highlights. In this section we incorporate a problem-solving orientation, but vision must not be left behind, and a balance kept.

When thinking about developing a change strategy, the following rules of thumb can help:

- *Who?*   Build a team with a wide range of role partners, who display overall a willingness to work and take a viable level of risk.
- *What?*   Choose more than one thing – 'light many fires' – with a promising chance of success.
- *When?*   Capture the moment, by exploiting any opportunity that arises, but do not expect improvement to be instant.
- *Where?*   Start where the system is and stay well grounded in knowledge of the particular school (rather than ideas from Mars).
- *Why?*   To learn and to improve everyone's quality of life in school.
- *How?*   Work with an optimistic bias and a light touch, avoiding being flooded by the conflictual aspects, and building resistances as you go.

Principles in improvement at the 'whole-school' level

- Remember that this level is important because it provides the overall context, not because it provides the comprehensive detail.
- Work on the overall dimensions which are key to the context: proactivity, collaboration, community and learner autonomy.
- Remember to appreciate what is currently successful.
- Develop mechanisms for learning more about how your school behaves at this level, with problem-solving processes appropriate to what is learned.
- Recognize that most effective school improvement comes through teamwork.

What is the range of alternatives?

Actions at the whole-school level are not always major organizational changes. Tim Brighouse tells a story of a small secondary school in Birmingham, where there was concern about the rate of exclusion and possible disaffection among pupils. The staff of about 40 composed a list of the pupils they were most worried about: there were about 60 at the first attempt. They reduced this list to the point that each member of staff was allocated to one pupil. The teacher's task was then simple and manageable: it was to make a little extra effort to recognize the pupil in question, by saying 'hello' on the corridor, occasionally asking how things were going, and so on. These simple means of increasing affiliation led to a significant decrease in exclusions.

The range of alternatives is considerable, since schools vary so much one from another. We offer here an indicative sample of examples in order to stimulate thinking. But our strong belief is that a good collaborative team of teachers will come up with better and more appropriate ideas for their particular school, using the four headings we have developed.

Examples of interventions to enhance a proactive approach

- Regular reviews of the patterns of behaviour, informed by data which is available in the school.
- Setting up problem-solving teams, with appropriate status and resources, to work on delimited areas.
- Agreements to reduce the use of reactive measures.
- Conceptual reviews of the ideas in use for improving behaviour.

Examples of interventions to enhance a collaborative school

- Improved connections which de-privatize teaching, e.g. co-teaching, mentoring, paired observation.

- Improved communication structure for exchanging successful ideas.
- Improving the collaborative climate of existing teacher meetings.
- Reviewing and enhancing the time which teachers have to meet and talk and conduct professional learning exchanges.
- Developing collaborative approaches to classroom problem-solving.

Examples of interventions to enhance a community school

- Discussing and broadcasting a clearer shared purpose.
- Valuing connections outside the classroom.
- Attending to students' induction and affiliation needs.
- Improving the resources for developing good staff relations.

Examples of interventions to enhance learner autonomy

- Eliciting learners' evaluations of and reflections on positive behaviour and learning.
- Use of active and collaborative approaches to learning.
- Training in project work.
- Developing approaches for learners to learn about learning.
- Promoting the skills of independent group work.
- Developing resources to support independent learning.

Clarify the patterns of difficulty

Any discussion of difficult behaviour is likely to be improved by regard to data, of whatever sort is available. Data can ensure that the conversation does not dwell at the emotional level. It can also help clarify the appropriate focus for work, which is not always the one which easily presents itself. For example, an outer London school set up a monitoring exercise for a week, with some staff privately hoping that the results would bring about a change in break-time schedules and duties. In fact, only 2 per cent of disruptive incidents occurred outside lesson time, and 33 lessons during the week were disrupted for their full duration. Thus the monitoring led to an examination of curriculum suitability, alongside staff INSET in classroom management and in pastoral care.

In recent years schools have moved from being almost data-free zones, to being overloaded with data, often of unhelpful varieties. So we are not suggesting an addition to this trend. Rather we suggest that there is often data which exists already in a school, but which has not been examined for the patterns which it contains. So it may be important to ask '*What data do you presently have in your school which provides evidence on patterns at the organizational level?*'

Typical answers include:

- referrals to head of year or others – analysed by pupil, teacher, sub-ject, time
- school incident book
- withdrawal room use – analysed by subject, gender, ethnicity, over time, sites
- school attendance data – analysed by year, tutor group, etc.
- lesson attendance data – analysed by subject, time, etc.
- tutor group 'travelling log'
- exclusions – analysed by tutor group, gender, ethnicity, etc.
- inspector's reports (local and national).

If we then go on to ask '*What other methods could you use to collect further data/information?*', there may be creative suggestions such as:

- questionnaires to staff
- informal surveys on an occasional basis
- structured reviews when the whole staff meet
- using a team or other meeting to collect perspectives
- observation – of a range of contexts: corridors, lessons, break-time
- pupil pursuit – to experience the overall profile of a pupil day
- individual reviews of groups conducted with the tutor
- questionnaires to pupils – incidence of disruptive behaviour, bullying, etc.
- relational database of incidents.

Some issues in collecting/handling such data are worth anticipating:

- It requires staff to adopt a broader-than-individual perspective.
- It is data which needs to be analysed more than one way: by pupil, by teacher, by day, etc.
- It can take time to collect.
- It may explode some myths in the school (e.g. which of the staff are experiencing difficulty and which are not).

Choosing what to work on first

There is no single way to promote development once you have recog-nized the connectedness between matters affecting school behaviour. When choosing where to start, it is not a 'do-or-die choice'. But by the time you have analysed the important dimensions of your school, and started to gather some information on the patterns, it is probably time to propose a development. Remembering that planned change in schools more often conforms to the description 'Ready, Fire, Aim', rather than the rational 'Ready, Aim, Fire', the key attitude to adopt is to try something and learn from it.

A moment's reflection on how your school changes might be fruitful.

Heller (1985) pointed out some of the ways in which different schools approach change. Some have a history of being adaptive and reflective: others are cautious and easily withdraw from change. A third group are energetic and pioneering, whereas a fourth group of schools are assertive and determined. If any of these terms seem to identify important features of your school, then it can be useful to tune your ideas and your approach to change to match that of the school.

Given the findings of research regarding change at this level, an early task will be to compose a working group or project group. The classic pitfall is to compose a group which consists of interested and enthusiastic staff. This risks creating a polarization – the 'keenies' and the rest – and could create perceptions of a clique. Instead the work group needs to include members from all teams and all points of view. It may test the staff skills of working together (the very skills we say pupils lack), but it is essential for a proper whole-school result. Members of a project group should not be asked to 'represent' the section of the school in which some of their work occurs, since this overstates formal roles and divisions, and can lead to 'fighting their corner'. But they should be asked to communicate to and fro the issues, discussions and ideas which emerge.

By this stage the initial review can be started, in which the group (using creative communication with all members of the school community) combines an audit with a collection of improvement possibilities. Utilizing the ideas and examples of interventions in this chapter, it becomes possible to ask 'Is this already happening in the school?' and 'What would be appropriate to enhance this in the school?', from which a manageable set of priorities for development would eventually be selected.

The working group will perhaps soon encounter, or indeed may contain, some of the forces against change at this level. A significant one which we encounter is indicated when colleagues say they do not like title of this chapter: 'How does your school behave?' 'It's not the school that behaves', they say, 'it's the pupils', and in so doing they disempower themselves. This point of view is often constructed around a very understandable fear of being blamed, which sets up a disposition against looking at how we contribute to the picture. It is sometimes associated with the appeal to not complicate matters and just get on with a quick fix – if this is the scenario then it is likely that later on you might recognize that such colleagues have no real intention of implementing the very fix they asked for.

Having considered the range of alternatives from the conceptual base of this chapter, we will close with comment on some of the common approaches which are currently found in UK schools, and consider when (and when not) they may form part of the range. In principle our view is that any interventions are useful to the extent that they enhance one or more of the four headings we have used above.

Packages, Assertive Discipline and all that

One of the alternatives which a number of schools consider is the package 'Assertive Discipline'. Such consideration is often triggered by an enthusiastic recommendation from a local adviser/inspector, or even from a government White Paper which seems to endorse or advertise this package.

In different hands it is different things: some may focus on the stages of teacher reactions, others may focus on negotiated classroom codes. But what impact does it have? In the USA, from whence it came, the interesting possibility has been raised that teachers *think* it improves matters, but observations do not confirm this:

> In summary, studies of Assertive Discipline show consistent evidence of effects on teachers' perceptions of various aspects of discipline, including reduced problem behaviors. However the evidence suggests only a small effect on teacher behaviour itself. Evidence for effects on student behaviour and attitudes is not supportive of Assertive Discipline training; that is, more studies found no effects, or mixed and negative effects, than found that Assertive Discipline training resulted in improved student behaviour and attitudes.
>
> (Emmer and Aussiker, 1989, p. 116)

In the UK, early studies which focused on the element which trained in the appropriate use of praise, indicated teachers increasing on this and children increasing levels of on-task behaviour. However, during a follow-up phase reductions in both of these were evident (Ferguson and Houghton, 1992). Later studies in 15 classrooms of five British primary schools show that on average teacher approval increased and teacher disapproval decreased, student on-task behaviour increased and the frequency of disruptive behaviour decreased. However, when analysed by individual teacher and class, there was not one of the 15 where the time trends in these four measures of teachers' and students' behaviour changed significantly (Nicholls and Houghton, 1995). Studies by teachers involved in courses we have run often indicate that the effects of this package are short-lived, especially if it is poorly introduced as a solution to everything. None the less we need to be clear about what it can help with, and under what conditions.

Although such a package may be presented by its enthusiastic proponents as 'one size fits all', this is unlikely to be realistic given the great variety in our schools. We prefer to encourage a diagnostic view that specifies the conditions in which it might be useful and the conditions when it is not. So, Assertive Discipline can be useful when:

• some teachers regularly get involved in long drawn-out disciplinary interactions with some pupils

- a school has lost its ordinary sense of routineness and it needs to regain some predictability (but it must soon go beyond this in order to achieve well)
- pupils and teachers need to discuss and review the rules of a class-room (but both parties must be involved).

Assertive Discipline is not useful when:

- used as the sole intervention or in an automatic manner, i.e. without using good professional interpretation (it can become an escalation system)
- it implies that compliance brings improvement, and encourages teachers to focus on being disciplinarians, which has been show to relate to ineffective teaching
- it diverts attention from other important aspects which influence class-room behaviour, such as the curriculum.

Overall we feel an affinity for the strong critique raised by writers such as Kohn (1996): although the originators of these approaches may sug-gest that their core purpose is to improve communication, they are often used in an attempt to increase compliance – pupil compliance and teacher compliance. An additional angle on Assertive Discipline is offered by considering the effect of the scheme on teachers. They are presented with a series of staged responses which should be clear to them and to pupils: departures from the publicized school rules are responded to by moving to the next stage of response, not by discussion of the situation or the generation of new solutions.

This scheme has a considerable parallel with some very famous stud-ies by Stanley Milgram (1963; 1992). Volunteer adults were involved in an experiment which apparently involved them giving electrical shocks to another person when they did not learn. As these experiments pro-gressed the volunteers gave increasingly severe shocks, and over 60 per cent ended up giving shocks on a scale which marked them as above the dangerous level. Although these volunteer 'teachers' often protested – especially when bangs or shouts were heard from the 'learner' in the adjoining room, they usually gave up their protests when the experi-menter said 'please continue: the experiment requires it'. In understand-ing how ordinary adults could obey instructions and engage in behaviour which appalled and distressed them, two factors are crucial. First, the power of the social situation in which this all occurred: second, the fact that they had started on this series of staged shocks meant that at any one point there was no significant extra reason to stop, especially in the face of 'the experiment requires'. So it is with schemes such as Assertive Discipline or Discipline for Learning. The net result of the series of stages is that teachers become more obedient, or rather their disobedience becomes ineffective. They are invited to become automata rather than professionals (or even humans).

Luckily, large numbers of teachers do not willingly or enthusiastically activate this sort of disciplinary aspect to their role. So in any school there will be teachers who do not agree with the allocation of resource to the introduction of such packages, including those who feel that the assumptions of such schemes conflict with their professional principles. On some occasion these staff represent a key resource in finding a better approach in the school.

School and the spaces between the classrooms

In considering the school as an organization we have now considered whole-school approaches to classrooms, and their limitation. The focus on classrooms is appropriate for what is known about whole-school improvement efforts, and will be continued in the next chapter. But the space between this chapter and the next represents the spaces between classrooms in the whole picture of the school. We refer to break-times, corridors, school grounds and so on, those situations in school life which are sometimes less supervised but are the arenas for many patterns in pupils' relations (Blatchford and Sharp, 1994).

A behaviour pattern of concern which often relates to these 'spaces between' is what we call bullying. It is interesting to note that pupils rarely use this term unless they have been expressly socialized to do so: they are more likely to use terms which describe the hurtful behaviour and which do not pick up on the reason we call it bullying, which is that an ongoing relation of dominance develops. Bullying is a fairly stable pattern of interaction, not a single incident. It therefore is not likely to respond to our strategies for dealing with single incidents. Instead we have to think about the interaction.

Definitional nit-picking could divert a school's energies away from acting: experienced workers in this field would say 'Bullying is long-standing violence, physical or psychological, conducted by an individual or group and directed against an individual who is not able to defend him/herself in the actual situation' (Roland, 1989, p. 143). Something which is raised by this definition is not always recognized: much bullying is carried out by a group or by individuals with a group audience. About 80 per cent of incidents are like this. Bullying can include a wide range of behaviours:

• physically aggressive: hitting, kicking, taking or damaging belongings
• verbal: name-calling, nasty teasing or spreading rumours
• indirect: deliberately leaving someone out or ignoring someone.

Concerted national attention to bullying developed in the UK in the early 1980s. After a flurry of surveys, definitional debates, policy-writing and so on, some experience of successful interventions emerged (Sharp and Smith, 1994). These give priority to focusing on the pupil peer culture in the school as a major part of a whole-school perspective. 'The behaviour of the wider peer group can influence the level of bullying behaviour which occurs. If the remainder of the peer group ignores or colludes with the bullying, it will increase. If they challenge it and support the victimised students, it will decrease' (Sharp, 1997, p. 3). Teachers are often the last people to find out that bullying has taken place. Most bullying is well hidden and carefully disguised. Many teachers underestimate the amount of bullying which takes place in and around school. This is why peer initiatives are so important (Sharp, 1996).

Students will be aware if a bullying relationship exists and are more able to take action against bullying. Peer disapproval of bullying behaviour is a powerful preventive force. Promoting an active and constructive response from bystanders helps. Students can be taught to take action against bullying by:

- showing disapproval
- supporting the victimized student
- reporting the incident to a member of staff.

Support networks at lunch-time and break-times can be built by setting up 'activity groups' run by students for students perhaps with games which anyone can join. For those students who feel left out and isolated, activity groups provide a safe and easy way of becoming involved with other students. More structured interventions incude peer counselling or mediation services. These approaches can be highly successful, if carefully planned, with clearly stated boundaries, support and review.

Levels of bullying vary considerably from school to school and the results of interventions also vary. The UK national anti-bullying project (see Smith and Sharp, 1994) found that whole – school interventions had a different effect in primary and secondary schools. In primary schools, there was an almost immediate effect on the levels of reported bullying. Some schools had decreases of up to 80 per cent. In schools which had done little to tackle the problem, bullying had stayed the same or had increased. In the secondary schools, reductions in levels of reported bullying decreased less dramatically. There was, however, a very marked increase in the number of students who would tell a teacher if they were being bullied and a similar increase in the number of students who would help someone who was being bullied. Two years later, those secondary schools which had continued to implement the policy actively had achieved reductions in levels of bullying and had continued to increase the supportive attitude of the students.

3

Improving classroom behaviour

Making sense of classrooms and classroom behaviour

It often seems that the classroom is one of the most talked-about contexts there is, at the same time as being one of the least understood. There is a great deal of simplified talk about what goes on in classrooms, much of it based on unrecognized assumptions. Such simplification becomes a significant problem when we consider how to improve classrooms, as simple prescriptions usually have little impact on them. We need ways of approaching classroom change which are equally as complex as the context.

If you were to select a person at random on the number 31 bus, and ask him or her to tell you how teaching should be organized in classrooms, the frightening fact is that you might receive an answer. Such an answer would be based on the fact that the person was once a pupil in a classroom. It might also reflect some of the media commentary about teaching, much of which is stimulated by the rhetoric of government and its agencies. These two perspectives have a worrying similarity in that both of them over-focus on two aspects: the first is the teacher, and the second is what they dislike about the teacher's performance. Such myopia does not get us far.

In this chapter we will build an alternative and more comprehensive focus on understanding the classroom situation and its effects, both on teachers and on pupils, before offering a range of frameworks for thinking about experiments to improve classroom behaviour. These frameworks are not offered as a set of prescriptions, but as some lines of action which depend on the diagnosis of the existing difficulty. The chapter finishes with some thoughts about broader methods of ensuring healthy classrooms.

Our perspective in this chapter is not that of the prevalent 'inside the person' explanations which were examined in Chapter 1 – neither for pupil nor teacher. Rather, we intend to recognize the importance of the context of behaviour, as in the chapters which precede and follow this one. An example of context in concrete terms was given by the Governor of a New York prison who was worried about the amount of fighting between inmates. The strategy of 'change the person', by putting fighters on a bread and water diet, seemed ineffective, as was the more liberal version of talking to fighting inmates to persuade them into better behaviour. The problem was finally solved by calling in a bricklayer, who rounded off the walls at the junctions of corridors – these had been identified as the situations where fighting broke out, when poor visibility led to surprise encounters. Perhaps this example is over-concrete, as it focuses so much on the physical aspects, and we know that situations are more than that. So, before we examine some of the specific and observable aspects of classrooms, it is also important to consider the meanings which may attributed to this context.

Images of classrooms

It is interesting and illuminating to ask yourself and to ask your colleagues the following question: 'What situation that is *not* a classroom is most like a classroom in your view?' In our experience this brings forward important trends and particulars. Many people find the question difficult to answer, which may reflect the uniqueness of the classroom situation in our society. Trends we have observed include that teachers in primary schools are more likely to answer 'a family' than are teachers in secondary schools, while the latter are more likely to offer situations such as theatre, or church, thereby reflecting the performance and audience aspects, and the traditional approaches to audience control. We suggest that teachers with these images of classrooms are more likely to engage in one-to-many interactions, expect to be listened to because of their role, and see their job as conveying a message. On the other hand, a different image was conveyed by a teacher in a Richmond school who answered 'an office': he described a situation where everyone came in each day knowing their roles and working relations, and what they aimed to achieve. Again a teacher who answered 'a restaurant' brought to attention her view of offering pupils a range on the menu, and indeed of changing the menu over time. Another teacher who answered 'an aeroplane' not only highlighted the physical aspects in her school where the desks had been placed in pairs, but also the role aspects of the hostess answering the call bell in this setting. Finally, a student teacher who wrote an essay likening classrooms to prisons, with no hope of alternatives, failed the course!

Clandinin (1985) describes a teacher's image of 'the classroom as home' showing how this embodies personal and professional experiences, and how in turn the image is expressed in her classroom practices. Bullough (1991) has shown how metaphors reflect conceptions of teaching, and how these evolve through student teaching, maintaining motivation on the journey. Connelly and Clandinin (1994) illustrate how the telling and writing, retelling and rewriting of teachers' and students' stories results in changes in teaching practices, while Bullough and Stokes (1994) explore the analysis of personal teaching metaphors as a means of facilitating professional development.

Teachers are major orchestrators in making classrooms into whatever they become, and within some broad trends, the variety of what they construct is considerable. The usefulness of identifying one's image of a classroom goes beyond mere illumination. It can be a route to significant improvement. If teachers are given the time and support to unearth their current images, they may also see good reason to move on to other images which are more sympathetic to the teacher role, more enhancing of pupil autonomy and more appropriate to the twenty-first century. Transformational change does occur on occasion, especially if a teacher's preferred image of classrooms is at stake. A teacher we met in Birmingham told us that she had changed her approach to teaching overnight: on being asked how she became the exception to the rule about classroom change being generally slow, she said that in her case a 'pupil pursuit' of a class she taught led her to vow that she would never again contribute to such a passive picture for pupils. She decided to pursue her preferred image of a classroom much more actively after that experience.

Understanding the classroom context

The classroom is measurably one of the most complex social situations on Earth. This statement is not made in order to mystify anything: quite the opposite – it makes sense of why simplistic approaches to classroom improvement do not work. For example, the tendency to focus on the teacher and to use oversimple descriptions of teachers does not fit the facts. Decades ago Ryans (1968) applied multiple psychometric measures to a sample of over 6,000 teachers and related them to assessments of their classroom work. Teachers receiving a uniformly high assessment of their classroom behaviour turned out to be those with the highest frequency of involvement in avocational (non-work) activities (Ryans, 1968, p. 393). There are two responses to these findings: one is to say 'Yes I can explain why teachers who do more at the weekends perform better in classrooms . . .'; the other is to say that such studies took a too-personal focus on the teacher, and missed the point by not analysing the context. If you only focus on the teacher you will get spurious perspectives.

Instead we use the fact that all our behaviour relates to context. This principle, often forgotten, was introduced in Chapter 1 and may be summed up by the statement: $B = f(p.s)$. Behaviour is a function of the person and the situation. Each human being has a unique profile of responses and approaches which vary across the situations he or she meets. A teacher who behaves in one way in classroom A may not do so in classroom B, and not in the staffroom, or at the pub. Sadly when a difficulty arises, all the focus may be on classroom A, rather than on the variety, range and exceptions. As we shall see in detail in the next chapter, similar considerations apply to pupils, whose behaviour varies in important ways across learning situations and social situations in and out of school.

So if we intend to focus on the context where teachers and pupils spend most of their school time, and in which the majority of difficulties in most schools are experienced – the classroom – it will be important to recognize some of the unique and influential aspects of that setting. The following derives from the work of Walter Doyle (1980; 1986a; 1986b; 1990).

Characteristics of the classroom situation

1 *Classrooms are busy places.* Teachers can be engaged in 1,000 interactions a day, sometimes more. It is very difficult to name a comparable job

on this dimension: perhaps air traffic controllers cope with comparable complexity, although their job makes less personal demands. Teachers make a non-trivial decision in the classroom every two minutes. One result of this for the teacher can, of course, be tiredness, especially for the beginner teacher or, if they do not find means of coping with the busyness, stress.

This feature also draws to our attention the fact that because events happen fast teachers learn to act fast: their appraisal and decision-making in classrooms is rapid. Even so, every event cannot be reflected on in depth, so the development of *routines* is another feature of classroom life which helps cope with the busyness of the situation. Some routines may embody poor practice as far as pupil learning is concerned, but the classroom situation makes such demands for routinisation.

For the pupils in this busy environment it is apparent (and confirmed by numerous classroom interaction studies) that the amount of individual attention they receive with the teacher in a day is likely to be only a few minutes and probably highly interrupted. The way in which we conceptualize learning in classrooms must take this into account by not implying that pupils learn only when interacting with teachers. The social skills of this busy situation are key to pupils being able to make the best of it: they have to get used to being one of many, especially when it comes to adult attention, and this can demand extra skills of being able to wait, or finding other sources of help. We often feel that more explicitness about these social skills and their development would relieve many difficulties in classrooms.

2 *Classrooms are public places.* This statement is meant in two ways. First, classrooms are public in the general sense that many people have a view or opinion on classrooms and how they ought to operate. Second, classrooms are public in that a teacher's and a pupil's behaviour is generally highly visible to all the other members in the event.

The implication of the first is that the teacher is at the centre of a number of people's expectations – parents, colleagues, head, local authority, central government and, of course, pupils. In the unlikely event that these various expectations are in broad agreement with each other, the teacher will probably feel strongly supported in her or his job. It is more likely that disagreements exist and the teacher feels in a state of 'role strain'. Resolving role strain can be accomplished in a number of ways, each with its own costs and benefits – a classic has been the strategy of isolating role performance from view by the conflicting parties: this leads to the phenomenon of classroom as a castle, with paper over the windows to the corridor.

The implications of the second sense of publicness are various: teachers may feel that they are 'on stage' to some degree and have to develop an approach which blends the public and the personal. Teachers may act towards one pupil with the intention of affecting others in the audience – the 'ripple effect' – but mainly teachers adopt a focus toward groups of pupils (whole class or less). This group focus grows out of the imbalance in numbers in the classroom and also serves to cope with the busyness of the situation.

Pupils learn to experience much public evaluation of their work and behaviour and they adopt a variety of strategies in the face of this: strategies to work out what answer teacher wants, strategies to assess whether teacher is being fair in her or his evaluations, especially when they are public, and so on. Some studies suggest that teachers give public evaluations of pupils every few minutes. Pupils learn to be treated as a member of a group which is not always of their choosing, and in turn may adopt a group approach toward affecting others – including, on occasion, their teacher.

3 *Classroom events are multidimensional.* There is a wide variety of purposes, interests and goals represented by the different personnel in a classroom. The teacher may have thoughts about the staff meeting this evening, or the mortgage: the pupils may have thoughts about what is on television or what someone said to their friend. In the middle of this, teaching and learning takes place. Personal–social aspects of pupils' and teachers' lives are always affecting classroom life.

Even when we focus on the learning dimension alone the statement still applies. The classroom contains a multiplicity of information sources – books, worksheets, displays, other visuals, as well as all the verbal and non-verbal behaviour of teachers and pupils – and these sources generally do not all refer to the same thing. The information from multiple sources is sometimes incompatible, and sometimes inconsistent, so that skills of selection are crucial for learners. This skill is even sometimes required in order to handle the ambiguities in a learning task.

For the teacher an implication is that they need to manage events on a multiplicity of dimensions: knowing subject, appraising students, managing classroom groups, coping with emotional responses to events, establishing procedures, distributing resources, encouraging thinking, keeping records and so on. With these tasks all affecting each other the result may feel overwhelming on occasion. Effective teachers accept and mediate this multidimensionality. Sometimes they engage it explicitly in their classroom management, through references to what they are aware of going on elsewhere, and sometimes in their subject, through links to daily life.

For pupils this multidimensional environment means that on the occasion when they intend to engage in academic work they need to display considerable skills in selecting what is salient information and what is not, especially when attempting to identify the demands of a task. These are not usually the skills which are referred to when identifying academic achievement.

4 *Classroom events are simultaneous.* The multiple events in the classroom do not occur in a step-by-step fashion but simultaneously, especially from the teacher's point of view. One group is happily working away, another group wants attention for something, and meanwhile someone is climbing out of the window. Teachers attend to numerous aspects at the same time: the pace of work, the sequencing of pupil contributions, the distribution of pupils attended to, the accuracy of pupil contributions, the development of the argument and so on, while at the same time monitoring work involvement levels, other pupil behaviours and external events.

This has at least two implications for teachers. First, it is important to exercise the skill (at least apparently) of being able to monitor more than one aspect at once. This is sometimes described as the 'eyes in the back of the head' phenomenon. Second, it follows that teachers may exercise a choice as to which aspect to respond to and which to ignore. The style of operation of this choice can have critical effects and can make the difference between a 'smooth' teaching performance which gives rise to a purposeful climate, and a 'lumpy' performance where the teacher seems controlled by events and appears to be 'chopping and changing'.

For the pupils the simultaneity of classroom events is not such a salient phenomenon since they may not intend to have a perspective on the whole situation and its events. However, the fact that it is salient for teachers can be exploited very effectively by those waiting for teacher's back to turn. Some pupils quickly learn the skills of avoiding teacher's monitoring.

5 *Classroom events are unpredictable.* In such a busy, multidimensional environment it is not possible to be in a position of predicting the course of events with a fine degree of accuracy. Despite teachers' proper professional attempts to predict how this group might respond to the material, or how long it might take, they know that there will be surprises, so they generally become skilled in recognizing and tolerating unpredictability.

Disruptive effects are easily generated by interruptions: the external ones (the window cleaner, the snowstorm) and the internal ones (the projector breakdown, the tannoy announcement). Routines in classroom life can be viewed as one attempt to engender predictability and reduce ambiguity. Nevertheless teachers perforce must be able to tolerate high levels of ambiguity in classroom life.

Pupils also have strategies for coping with unpredictability: their seeking every detail of what is expected in a task, searching for the answer teacher wants, requesting low-risk predictable tasks, and making teacher predictable through stereotype and labelling are examples. They all serve as attempts to reduce ambiguity.

This analysis helps us realize that the nature of classrooms demands that teachers exhibit high level skills, an ability to interpret situations and orchestrate learning. They often cannot describe these aspects, and sometimes feel hesitant to do so lest it divides them from the layperson. But their professionalism is founded on this complexity.

It also helps us recognize the poverty of those views which portray the classroom as a simple cause-and-effect situation, which offer a simple teacher-centred view, and which seem to imply that there is a prescription for successful teaching in all contexts. These views are common, but are positively dangerous as a basis for improving classrooms. They lead respectively to teachers feeling de-skilled when simple add-ons do not work, to classrooms not being places where students develop the skills to take responsibility for their learning, and to the creativity of the system being depressed. This can lead to teachers passing on prescriptions, which can in turn depress student performance.

This understanding of the classroom setting, its demands and constraints, accounts for other important phenomena. It helps us appreciate that teachers exchange, use, even create new practices daily as they face and resolve problems in the classroom. Large-scale programmes and curricula probably represent a small proportion of the everyday changes which teachers are making in their classrooms. Teachers decide whether their practices are valid from a range of bases, from personal feeling to scientific, with a tendency toward the former – the intuitive practitioner, feeling his or her way through. They are involved in recipe collecting and exchanging, traded on the basis of 'what worked for me' and 'what feels right'. The working assumption is that one practitioner cannot *tell* another something: they can only exchange experiences. Although teachers may seek information from a range of sources, this is highly dependent on availability and accessibility: peers in the same school become the most credible.

When it comes to improving classrooms from the perspective of difficult behaviour, this perspective also sets us up to examine more about the situation and how it is orchestrated than about individual incidents. Here we will consider significant differences in style of management, but before we do that it is instructive to register some widespread trends.

Surveys of teachers' views of troublesome behaviour in classrooms have been conducted in various phases and various places. Wheldall and Merrett (1988) surveyed 198 teachers in the West Midlands, asking them to identify the most troublesome behaviours from ten categories provided. Forty-seven per cent elected 'talking out of turn' (hereafter referred to as 'TOOT') followed by 25 per cent choosing 'hindering other children'

(HOC). For the most frequent troublesome behaviour, the results were similar: TOOT 55 per cent, HOC 21 per cent, with no other category above 10 per cent. When asked about the most troublesome behaviour of the particularly troublesome individuals, the results were TOOT 33 per cent, HOC 27 per cent. Houghton, Wheldall and Merrett (1988) surveyed 251 secondary teachers in the same area: the most frequent and troublesome classroom misbehaviours were TOOT 50 per cent and HOC 17 per cent. A modified survey of 70 nursery teachers found 55 per cent of teachers listing 'not listening', and concluded 'In nurseries where the work is much less formal, the same type of behaviours are seen to be trouble-some to teachers' (Merrett and Taylor, 1994, p. 293).

Further afield, in St Helena 50 returns from first and middle school teachers showed most disruptive behaviour: TOOT 42 per cent, facing away from work 25 per cent. The most common misbehaviours were TOOT 43 per cent, facing away from work 16 per cent. In particularly troublesome children, TOOT was most disruptive and most frequently occurring. (Jones, Wilkin and Charlton, 1995). In Singapore 89 primary school teachers rated the most disruptive behaviours as talking 26 per cent, and disturbing others 21 per cent, although interestingly 15 per cent chose nothing. The most commonly occurring misbehaviours for these teachers were: talking 42 per cent and facing away from work 13 per cent (Jones, Quah and Charlton, 1996).

In a similar vein, research carried out for the Elton Report (Gray and Sime, 1989) analysed questionnaire results from 2,500 secondary teachers and 1,050 primary teachers in England and Wales. Of the problem behaviours which teachers experienced, TOOT was again top of the list: 97 per cent of each group reported it occurring at least once during the week, with 53 per cent of secondary and 69 per cent of primary teachers report-ing its occurrence at least daily. Further, TOOT was identified as the prob-lem behaviour most difficult to deal with, and when asked to consider a particularly difficult class, the most difficult behaviour was TOOT. The same questionnaire was returned by 156 junior primary and 621 primary teachers in South Australia (Johnson, Oswald and Adey, 1993). The most common discipline problems were TOOT 30 per cent, HOC 38 per cent, and idleness and work avoidance 33 per cent. When asked to report on a difficult class, the behaviours which were difficult were the same.

The similarity in these results is striking, notwithstanding some inter-esting differences. What is the problem with TOOT? Why do teachers across the world report it with such regularity? There are two main response to these questions. The first is to address the behaviour, and to start with the most difficult pupils (who interestingly are not reported as displaying different types of difficult behaviour), and develop a method with them of reducing the behaviour. This is the behavioural approach, as most recently described by Anderson and Merrett (1997). Leaving aside for a moment the question of who will staff such a specialized intervention, the track record of behavioural approaches raises some doubts when implemented in the classroom: Bain, Houghton and Williams (1991) report that the frequency of the targeted teacher behaviour, such as 'teacher encouragement', can return to near-baseline levels after the intervention ends. Corrie (1997) adds an extra doubt about this approach, by demonstrating that the frequency of TOOT varies in classrooms, and by studying the classroom situation in which it occurs she found that different teachers had different views of that situation, their roles, their approaches to the group, to learning and so on. It was not to be reduced to a consideration of 'teacher skill'.

So an alternative response to the above surveys is to say that they tell us something important about the typical classroom situation, around the world. This would require us to consider the role of talk in classrooms, and how it may be best utilized in the service of learning, teachers' views on this, the organizational perceptions of classroom talk, and the degree to which the classroom curriculum encourages, supports and develops talk.

Why reactive approaches are not effective

In parallel with the findings about the reactive school (see Chapter 2), the reactive classroom is not effective for improving behaviour. As before, we take being proactive to mean anticipating potential difficulty, thinking ahead rather than waiting for problems to arise. In contrast, being reactive means only responding to current problems, and planning a response once they have arisen.

Many approaches focus on aspects of the teacher's response to unwelcome behaviour. These latter often reflect the question which may be heard in many unstructured teacher conversations about classroom difficulty: 'What do I do if . . . ?' or 'What do you do about . . . ?' The inherent risk is that of casting the teacher in a response-led role, which is an ineffective strategy in the classroom situation. It is a case of closing the stable door after the horse has bolted.

Responses to events do not provide the answer. They set the teacher on the back foot and can initiate a pattern of the teacher being run by events rather than of orchestrating purpose and momentum in the classroom. What is more, responses of the short variety do not work. Clarke *et al.* (1981; Gay and Parry-Jones, 1980) undertook a detailed analysis of the internal structure of disruptive incidents in classrooms, detailing the actions which initiated and terminated the incidents. The analysis demonstrated that 'soft' and discursive strategies were four times more likely to lead to an exit from the incident than were hard commands. O'Hagan and Edmunds (1982) demonstrated that apparently successful attempts to control disruptive conduct by intimidatory practice may have deleterious consequences in other ways, for example, on pupils' inclination to truant. So when we raise some aspects of teachers' responses later in this chapter, it is with recognition of their secondary importance to the wider aspects of classroom management.

The most effective element in reducing general classroom disruption is the teacher's skill in planning activities. This implication is supported by research findings such as those of Kounin (1977), whose extensive and detailed studies showed that the action which teachers took in response to a discipline problem had no consistent relationship with their managerial success in the classroom. However, what teachers did *before* misbehaviour occurred was shown to be crucial in achieving success, through a preventive focus which reduced difficulty. The teacher's ability to manage the classroom group through planned activities is a key element in developing constructive behaviour patterns.

So, with these contextual points in mind, we turn to consider difficult behaviour in classrooms and its improvement. For the reasons given we will not adopt reactive approaches, and will not fall into another available trap of focusing on deficits in teachers' 'classroom management skills'. There is not a meaningful consensus on what these are, and as Corrie (1997) has shown, any focus on the teacher would be better served by considering their knowledge and conceptions of classrooms. Instead, we take a first step of clarifying the picture of the difficulty.

Diagnosing classroom difficulty

Many 'solutions' which are proposed for difficult behaviour in classrooms are not based on a diagnosis of the situation. They are favourite solutions which may work but may not. For example, one source of advice may suggest that a teacher becomes more 'positive' and rewarding, another may propose that the differentiation of tasks needs attention, while another may want to alter the social relations. The list could easily go on, but we must ask the question, 'What is the basis for the advice?' In many cases it is an enthusiasm transferred from another situation, or in some cases it is an enthusiasm for a particular model for fixing a classroom. Given what we recognize about the complexity of the classroom, any advice which pre-selects a single aspect for focus is likely to work only as a matter of chance. Instead of this, we need to develop a way of being clearer about the difficulty and of matching the advice to that clearer picture. We will call this 'diagnosis', although we do not wish to stimulate medical connotations and the idea that a single organic cause will be found. Given the complexity and connectedness of classrooms, an 'accurate' linear diagnosis will not be forthcoming, but a narrowing of the focus will be achieved.

There are probably a number of dimensions along which classroom difficulty could be addressed. Given the importance of context in behaviour, we have chosen to order things in terms of how widespread in time and space the difficulty is. So diagnosing the *extent* of difficulty will develop a clearer focus. We recognize that this does not always happen in everyday conversation about classroom difficulty, since teachers are not practised in being specific. 'That class was awful today' is a comment which many of us will have heard (and may have used), but such a comment does not necessarily reflect an accurate analysis of the pattern of behaviour, and is likely to be an overstatement of the position. Given this, it is valuable to be more specific about the extent of difficulty, with the caveat that exaggerated comments are often delivered in the staffroom at breaktime, where it is not necessary to initiate immediate action (other than to continue stirring the coffee).

The challenge is to adopt a form of diagnostic thinking which will support us in spotting the patterns in the difficult behaviour.

The following questions attempt a starting diagnosis, and lead on to ideas and frameworks which may be useful in thinking about improvement of the behaviour patterns.

Is there a *particular* disaffection in this classroom? In other words is it restricted to particular times, places or persons?

If Yes, does the disaffection relate to:

1 Particular sorts of teacher–pupil interactions.
  Examine skills in handling conflict, avoiding
  escalations.   (sections A to G)
2 A particular *classroom* context.
  Analyse the physical, social and psychological
  features of this classroom.   (section H)
3 Particular *activities*.
  Analyse the design and message of these
  activities.   (section I)
4 A particular *subgroup* of pupils.
  Analyse the role of this group within the class
  and the roles of key members within the group.   (section J)

If No, is there a general disaffection in this class? In other words does it seem to involve most people and most occasions?

If Yes, does the disaffection relate to:

1 The *curriculum* offered. Is it appropriate for this class?
  Do pupils feel they achieve something valuable?   (section K)
2 The *profile of activities*. Is it engaging?
  Are pupils involved in the activities?   (section L)

---

3 The *responsibilities* in this class. Are they developed and shared?
  Are pupils involved in planning? (section M)
4 Classroom *rules*. Are they agreed, understood, accepted and used?
  Are pupils reviewing the success of this class? (section N)
5 The *climate*. Does it need review and improvement? (section O)
6 The sense of *community* in this classroom. Is it positive? (section P)

The sections which follow contain various suggestions for action (and inaction) on the part of a classroom teacher experiencing difficult behaviour. But at the outset let us be clear:

- Not all of these suggestions will be appropriate for your situation.
- Not all of these suggestions will be appealing to you as a teacher.
- Not all of these suggestions will 'work' – especially if we take that to mean producing obedience.

Anyone who felt they had to do *all* of what follows would be overwhelmed straight away. But if you use these suggestions to set off trains of thought about the situation you know and find difficult, and if you professionally select and modify the suggestions to your own situation, there may be some value gained. Clearly a series of considerations and possible lines of action is not a workbook of recipes.

If you let the diagnostic questions above lead you to some sections rather than others, then the order of the sections which follow is unimportant. They are certainly not in order of importance. Beginning with the most immediate considerations, what to think about and do in a difficult interaction, might appear to promote a 'What do I do if they do X?' mentality, which is exactly the sort of reactive approach which does not work. Somewhat better would be to ask the proactive question 'How can I create a classroom where these things don't happen?', which is considered in the latter sections. These later suggestions are not any less immediate because they appear later – we can start changing our classroom climate tomorrow, for example. Nevertheless we put incidents first, in order to speak to the concerns of the teacher, perhaps tired and frustrated, who has a focus on particular individuals and incidents – let us consider them first before moving to the wider scale and equally immediate matters of classroom patterns and classroom community.

Frameworks and ideas for improving classroom behaviour patterns

The first few sections have a common theme: how a teacher can develop their choice of response to a difficult incident, as opposed to feeling that they have to react in ways which are not improving the situation. It is not surprising that in the busy classroom situation, quick reactions are made: the problem arises when these contribute to the escalation of a troublesome incident. We all find ourselves in situations where we feel we have little choice, but by thinking about the situation and the message we most wish to convey a new range of alternatives can develop.

A   Styles of responding

Consider the following classroom situation: Timothy grabs Rosemary's ruler and appears to hide it from her.

Consider the following options for the teacher:

(1)   'Timothy, stop being childish and give back Rosemary her ruler.'
(2)   'Timothy we ask before borrowing in this classroom.'
(3)   'Timothy, you're quite able to get on with your work, so return Rosemary's ruler and let her do the same.'

These three simple options have both similarities and differences. They are similar in that they all indicate to Timothy that the teacher has noticed his behaviour and decided it is inappropriate. In that sense they may all serve to mark a boundary on behaviour. But they also have differences:

(1)   has elements of judging the person, negatively.
(2)   points to an agreement previously made.
(3)   refers to roles and responsibilities in learning.

The impact of these different styles, if generalized over time, can be quite marked. Style (1) can be counterproductive in terms of improving behaviour because it may build up resentments: it may be the style of the 'deviance-provocative teacher' (see section G). Style (2) can be effective if it is set against a background of making and reviewing agreements regarding classroom behaviour. Style (3) makes the important link with what we aim to achieve in classrooms, it reaffirms our purpose.

 Think about your responses to small-scale incidents. What messages do they convey:

  • about the pupil?
• about the classroom climate and control?
• about the purposes in your classroom?

But style (1) is quite prevalent in our classrooms. The most frequently occurring teacher comments are very brief: 'Stop it' and 'Shut up!'

B Teachers' ways of conveying to pupils that behaviour is inappropriate

When things are going well, the communication between teachers and pupils is complex and reflects shared meanings which have developed between them. For example, the teacher who, without looking up from the work she is checking with a pupil, says 'someone's being silly' and two pupils at the back of the room stop the behaviour they are involved in – because they know and can interpret the informal rules of that class-room. On another occasion in another classroom, the same comment might be ineffective as the teacher has not built up shared meaning with a class with the result that their ways of conveying the inappropriacy of behaviour are not successful.

Hargreaves, Hester and Mellor (1975) identified the following 11 teacher strategies:

1 Descriptive statement of the deviant conduct: 'You're taking a long time to settle down'.
2 Statement of the rule which is being invoked: 'Rulers aren't for fighting with', 'When I'm talking no one else talks'.
3 Appeal to pupil's knowledge of the rule: 'You know you're meant to write it in the book'.
4 Command/request for conformity to the rule: 'Shut up', 'Put that away'.
5 Prohibitions: 'Don't', 'Stop that'.
6 Questions: 'Are you listening?', 'What's going on over there?'
7 Statement of the consequences of the deviant conduct: 'I won't bother to read if you go on like this', 'Someone will get hurt if this equipment is left lying here'.
8 Warnings and threats: 'I'm going to get annoyed', 'You'll be in detention', 'I'll send you to the head'.
9 Evaluative labels of the pupil and her or his conduct: 'Stop behaving like a baby', 'Don't be daft'.
10 Sarcasm: 'We can do without the singing', 'Have you retired?'
11 Attention-drawers: 'Sandra!', 'girls!', '5C!'

If we ask the question 'Are some of these strategies more effective than others?' we have to recognize that all of them can be effective in some situations in the short term. However, strategies 2 and 7 are worthy of our attention since they achieve two goals: they signal that the behaviour is unwanted and they communicate the rule which the teacher sees as being broken. As such they are likely to have the most effective long-term contribution, especially in a classroom where the communication of informal rules seems to have been ineffective.

Within this theme we do not want to convey an image of successful classrooms as rule-bound environments: neither pupils nor teachers find that motivating, and the occasions when rules are relaxed are often memorable for building relationships. One of pupils' criteria for judging teachers is 'can he have a laugh?' (Gannaway, 1984). However, breaking rules is most meaningful when someone knows what the rule is that is being broken.

 Can you monitor the clarity of rule communication in your classroom, and adjust if necessary?

C Responding to aggression – assertively

Aggression may comes in a number of forms – verbal, indirect, and so on. Direct physical aggression towards a teacher is comparatively rare: reported and recorded non-accidental injuries involve one-third of 1 per cent of teachers (see data cited in Department for Education and Science, 1989).

When faced with direct aggression, the two main responses are 'fight' (returning the aggression) or 'flight' (non-assertion). These may seem natural or, indeed, sensible in evolutionary terms. However, their cumulative effect in a classroom is unlikely to promote a constructive set of relationships. It is possible to develop a new response – learning to respond to aggression assertively. In this mode a teacher can retain more control of his or her own behaviour, and therefore go beyond the more basic 'fight or flight'.

When people start to consider and develop more assertive responses in their repertoire, two connected things become noticeable. First, their predictions – they often predict that they will get a violent reaction to their assertive response. This is inaccurate, as anyone who goes beyond this fear to experiment with assertive responses will tell you. But this fearful prediction can stop a few people ever reaching the experimental stage. This is the second point: our predictions shape our range of behaviour – this can be limiting, as implied above, or it can be in an expanding fashion, where our predictions support a wider range of action options. It is useful, therefore, to practise identifying one's own predictions, especially those small 'inner voices' which speak in moments of difficulty.

 Remember or anticipate a situation where you were on the receiving end of someone else's aggression. Try to notice your own 'inner dialogue'. This may be very brief, but can have strong effects, both on how you subsequently feel and on your range of possible behaviour. You can practise spotting this and its effects. Here are some examples:

Inner dialogue	Possible feelings	Possible response
1 'Who does s/he think s/he is?'	Anger	Aggression
2 'How could he behave like that in my classroom?'	Hurt	Non-assertion
3 'This looks nasty: I'd better go along with it'	Fear	Non-assertion
4 'He's getting annoyed but I've seen this before'	Calmness	Assertion

 Does one of the above 'ring bells' for you? In other words is it more commonly part of your repertoire than the others? Can you rehearse some new inner dialogue more along the lines of example 4?

Professionals who behave confidently and who give the impression that things are under control are less likely to be assaulted or to witness assaults (Poyner and Warne, 1988).

D How can I get myself to react less?

Adopting a more calming inner dialogue will help to ensure that difficulties do not escalate, and is part of becoming less reactive. This takes practice. Here it is worth considering the very fast sequence which occurs when we are faced with any incident. It starts with the lower part of the brain firing off some very quick feelings. Then follow, we hope, the higher parts of the brain which bring in a range of considerations and previous experiences. Finally, we decide what to do and act. As Goleman (1996) has clarified, emotionally intelligent behaviour operates a sequence as shown in Figure 3.1.

Figure 3.1   Three stages in emotionally intelligent behaviour

The problem with some of our reactions is that the 'think' stage is by-passed, so that what we do is driven by what we feel.

 Developing new responses will also test out our beliefs. Sometimes we might impose inflexibilities on ourselves by holding particular beliefs. Test yourself by noticing how you feel about

this comment from a headteacher in the west of England: 'The individual with the greatest flexibility of thought and behaviour can and generally will control the outcome of any interaction.'

 There are various approaches to reducing our reactivity. We could:

- deliberately make more of a gap between the Feel and the Do:
  - count to ten (or less)
  - consider more than one option.

  It can be useful to be open-handed about this, saying what is going on as you are doing it, for example: 'I'll count to five now, and consider whether it would be best to do X or Y.' This can be very effective for demonstrating that you retain control – of yourself first and of your role.
- spot the inner voices which make you most reactive, i.e. the thoughts which serve to perpetuate feelings rather than move on from them. Examples which might keep you stuck in reactive mode could include:
  - 'That Terry is a mean little blighter.'
  - 'He's always trying to take advantage of me.'
  - 'She shows no respect for me or for anyone.'
- Occasionally try something counterintuitive to break the pattern:
  - 'Wayne, what a nice pair of shoes, are they new?'
  - 'Nigel, I want you to walk round the classroom shouting.'

Brown (1986) has indicated how there are occasions when being paradoxical with a pupil actually stimulates them to exercise more of their self-control.

E What the pupil says next

There are some classic responses which pupils give when teacher has suggested they are doing something inappropriate. These were identified in the 1950s by Sykes and Matza (1957) and remain alive and well now:

- 'It wasn't me', 'It was X's fault' (denial of responsibility).
- 'We were only having a laugh', 'It didn't hurt' (denial of injury).
- 'It was only Y', 'He deserved it' (denial of the victim).
- 'I bet you've done it', 'You let Z off' (condemning the condemners).
- 'It was important to show him . . .' (appeal to higher loyalties).

There are various ways in which you might perceive these responses, each of which could lead you to different paths for your next response:

- as 'excuses'
- as testing you out
- as the sort of responses which self-respecting people give when accused.

 What will our next response be? Here are three types of possibilities:

- *Escalate*? For example, 'Don't give me those excuses' or 'Don't speak to me like that'. There is good evidence that such responses do lead to matters escalating. Créton, Wubbels and Hoomayers (1989) and Admiraal, Wubbels and Korthagen *et al.* (1996) have highlighted the vicious cycles when teacher and pupils symmetrically intensify each other's behaviour. Remember that giving hard commands can lead to hard responses from pupils.
- *Hostile*? 'You should be ashamed of yourself.' Well, let us hope that shame is not what pupils take away from their classroom experience. This sort of response does not give the pupil room to save face, and to wind down when they have been playing the wind-up game with teachers. As Rogers (1992) points out, students who seem to want the last word are often concerned about how they manage in front of their peers.
- *Passive*? 'Why are you doing that?' That is a question to which there is no real answer, and we do not want it anyway. We want the difficulty to reduce and constructive working relations to resume. Asking this sort of question can give pupils a wonderful opportunity to side-track you with lots of creative answers to your question.

Preferable to these three responses is something which is both assertive (not aggressive) and non-escalatory, something which brings attention back to the important matters of the classroom and productive relations for learning. Perhaps 'That's as may be – now let's get this activity done'.

Some of the skills in asserting yourself, as described by Dickson (1982) are:

- give a clear statement of what you want: 'I want you to return to your table.'
- stick to your statement, repeating it as necessary.
- deflect the other person's responses, the ones which may undermine your statement, for example irrelevances or argumentation, perhaps by prefacing your restatement with a short recognition of their view: 'I've heard your reason for looking at the fish, but I want you to return to your table.'

Rogers (1992) suggests that pupils often engage teachers in 'secondary behaviour' which diverts the teacher from their original concern of resuming activity. This could be any number of things: a grunt, a glance to a peer, a question – the potential is considerable. In this context assertiveness is appropriate, remembering that it is not about getting your own way but about practising clear communication within the rights and responsibilities of one's role.

F *Managing conflict*

Conflicts will happen, in classrooms as much as anywhere else. Conflicts are endemic in school life: that is not necessarily a problem – it is the way we handle them that matters. One of the most important orienting points is not to confuse conflict with aggression: such a view can lead to conflicts being swept aside or denied. Different sorts of conflicts you might meet include: (1) conflicts within yourselves, you want to carry on talking with a pupil at break and you also want to get some coffee; (2) conflicts between yourself and someone else, the class wants to see part of the video again but you want to move on; (3) conflicts between other people, some pupils are arguing about whose actions led to the experiment failing. It can be useful to clarify to yourself which type of conflict you are experiencing. Here we will comment on type (3) then (2).

When teachers find that difficult behaviour in a classroom is expressing conflicts between pupils, they sometimes say that they feel at a loss for how to improve matters. There are a number of background features which help to reduce conflict and to advance pupils' personal-social development (see, for example, Katz and Lawyer, 1994):

1 *Co-operation.* Helping children learn to work together and trust, help, and share with each other.
2 *Communication.* Helping children learn to observe carefully, communicate well, and listen to each other.
3 *Respect.* Helping children learn to respect and enjoy people's differences and to understand prejudice and why it is wrong.
4 *Expressing themselves positively.* Helping children learn to express feelings, particularly anger, in ways that are not destructive, and learn self-control.
5 *Conflict resolution.* Helping children learn how to resolve a conflict by talking it through.

When managing conflicts between others:

- Get the parties to talk in a structured way – one at a time – taking turns to speak and to listen.
- If appropriate, get both parties to take more distance on the situation by writing down how they see it.
- Get them to make suggestions for how to end the conflict.

- Treat it as a practical problem-solving exercise, rather than a moral lesson: 'what can we do to solve this?' rather than 'I want you to apologise right now'.
- Make sure that each person's proposal for resolving the conflict is put in clear practical terms, and that the other person has had a chance to indicate whether they agree to the proposal (Bach and Wyden, 1968).

A conflict ends when each person has aired their views, and they have questioned each other enough to ensure that this airing has been properly achieved.

 Have you tried a structured and practical approach to managing conflicts between others? What else would you add to the points above?

How would you vary the points above for the situation in your class?

When you're in a conflict with someone else:
- Keep it private – just between you
- Ask 'Is what has led to this really so important?'
- Avoid coming across as threatening
- Look for a new alternative, in which both can 'win'
- Help the other person to say more about his/her view of what's going on
- Explain your view of things clearly

G The deviance-provocative teacher and the deviance-insulative teacher

This is an idea about how teachers may vary in their handling of difficult incidents. We all vary, so it is not an idea for putting us into fixed categories.

When we are a deviance-provocative teacher (Jordan, 1974), we *believe* that the pupils we define as deviant do not want to work, and will do anything to avoid work. It is impossible to provide conditions under which they will work, so the pupils must change. Disciplinary interactions are a contest or battle – which we must win.

When we are a deviance-insulative teacher, we *believe* that these pupils really want to work, but that the conditions are assumed to be at fault. These can be changed and it is our responsibility to initiate that change. Disciplinary interactions relate to a clear set of classroom rules which are made explicit to the pupils.

The deviance-provocative teacher is unable to defuse situations, frequently issues ultimatums, and becomes involved in confrontations, whereas the deviance-insulative teacher allows students to 'save face', and avoids confrontations.

Thus the deviance-insulative teacher has some beliefs and responses which make up a 'virtuous cycle' in which behaviour goes well. Whereas the deviance-provocative teacher has some beliefs and responses which make up a 'vicious cycle' in which behaviour does not go well.

In lessons managed by the deviance-provocative teacher, deviant pupils are neglected other than for the many negative evaluative comments made about them. Pupils are referred to higher authority when they refuse to comply – which they do. The deviance-insulative teacher avoids favouritism, or other preferential treatment in lessons.

 Can you think of occasions when you have become deviance-provocative? What led to this happening? Can you think of occasions when you have become deviance-insulative? What led to this happening?
Are there any ways through which you can ensure more of the latter and less of the former?

H Skills in managing the classroom context

Creative teachers display many skills. Those included in the following framework relate to the particular complexities of the classroom which were outlined at the start of this chapter.

Teachers managing the classroom situation are:

1 managing the physical setting – layout, seating, resources, etc.
2 managing the social structure – groupings, working patterns, etc.
3 managing the psychological setting of the classroom:
    a handling the timing and pacing, developing effective routines;
    b giving a personal yet public performance, with a focus on group participation;
    c being aware of the multiple dimensions of classroom life, and showing it;

 To identify some useful pointers for your own action:
• Identify an occasion when a classroom you were managing created a positive, purposeful atmosphere. Apply the headings above to that example. What aspects of your classroom management went well?
• Now think of a less positive example where the behaviour concerns you. Apply these headings to that example. What aspects of your classroom management are highlighted? Identify two areas which it could be useful to develop in order to address your concern.

d managing more than one event at the same time, ignoring as appropriate;

e recognizing and tolerating the unpredictable nature of classroom life

This framework of headings can be useful on those occasions when it seems that difficult behaviour is associated with a particular classroom. As a precursor it can also be useful to think about our broad profile of skills.

 Is there a particular classroom which is causing you concern?

Here we use the term 'classroom' deliberately, since teachers sometimes tell us that they experience most difficulty in a particular room. 'They're fine during the rest of the week – it's just when we get into that room.' In this case it is useful to analyse the features of the classroom which this framework highlights:

1 *Physical setting*: layout of furniture, positioning of seats, resources, lighting, display, etc. (for a literature review see Weinstein, 1979). Do any of these seem linked to the difficulty? If so, can you experiment with some aspect? We have seen groups of teachers deconstruct and reconstruct the physical design of a classroom, rearranging everything which moves, in order to support the patterns of behaviour they seek. Managing the physical setting is one of the teacher's key skills, but not always exercised: they often de-skill themselves by saying that someone else would not like a change on this front – the cleaner, the colleagues, even the pupils.

The physical setting of a classroom also carries messages about ownership and purpose of that place. Review these in a classroom where difficulty is occurring. Are there positive signs of pupils and purpose in this room?

2 *Social structure*: the groupings of pupils, patterns of working together, rationales given, etc. (also the subject of a later review by Weinstein, 1991).

Classroom life is about being in groups, yet this aspect is often not analysed or developed. Broadly speaking, classrooms can be effective with any social structure in which a range of groups are used for learning and in which pupils learn about being in a group. Groupings which carry signs of devaluing some pupils (for example, so-called ability grouping) can lead to worsening patterns of behaviour. If you think that a particular way of grouping is related to difficult behaviour, you might consider a range of modifications. One teacher gave each pupil a playing card as they entered the classroom: large groups could be formed using the suits, small groups using the card values. This also carried the message that it was important to be able to work with anyone in the class. Regrouping of pupils can be quickly carried out by allocating a letter to each person in the current grouping and then composing new groups on the basis of the letters. The element of randomness is also useful as it demonstrates that teacher does not have some secret basis on which to rig the groupings. Teachers who involve pupils in thinking about groupings in this way will usually find that the groups work better.

The rationale for working in groups might be poorly communicated in some classrooms: reiterating that it is for getting on with the learning and for getting on with each other is necessary. Reteaching the skills of working together can be important.

3 *Psychological setting*: this is mainly managed through the type of activities in the classroom and the way they are conducted. Teachers actually manage activities rather than students, and as Doyle (1990, p. 351) remarks, 'if an activity system is not established and running in a classroom, no amount of discipline will create order'. Specific activities will be reviewed in the next section.

a) The busyness of the classroom is managed through timing and pacing of activities. Too few activities can lead pupils to seek diversion: too many can get them confused. The transitions between classroom activities can be unstable periods which need effective orchestration. They are well handled when preceded by some advance warnings: 'There are three minutes before we return to the whole group', 'We've been working on this experiment for ten minutes now so you should be about half-way through'.

b) The publicness of classrooms can create difficulties if it becomes exaggerated. In other words if everyone's behaviour, and especially any difficult behaviour, becomes the heightened focus for public attention. It is constructive to have private interchanges in the classroom, including with those pupils whose behaviour concerns you. Positive communications such as praise are more effective if handled privately. The sense of the classroom being a stage for everyone's performance declines as the relationships in a group develop, and as the focus returns to learning activities not persons.

c) The multidimensional nature of classroom life needs recognition. Those teachers who try to keep the rest of life firmly outside the door operate less effective classrooms. Instead of operating defensively in that way, the challenge is to acknowledge the rest of life and link it to the learning. This may mean giving a few moments to something which you know is engaging pupils' attention, and seeing what can be learned before moving on to the classroom agenda. More broadly a curriculum which has been related to the life experiences of pupils is a hallmark of authentic pedagogy, in which pupils are challenged to think, and to apply academic learning to important, real-world problems. Pupils who receive more authentic pedagogy learn more, regardless of social background, race, gender (Newmann, Marks and Gamoran, 1995).

d) The simultaneity of classroom events demands a key skill from the teacher, that of selective ignoring. Effective teachers are effective at deciding what to overlook. They give a 'smooth' performance, which maintains a sense of momentum, and conveys the sense that they are steering the events. By contrast, the teacher who does not use such skills effectively gives a 'lumpy' performance, responding to something here then something there, so that momentum is lost and the events seem to be in control. Perhaps in a classroom where difficulty has developed, a teacher can find their sensitivity heightened towards that difficulty, and as a result exercises the skills of selective ignoring less well. More broadly, there are occasions when our own approaches to managing the classroom constitute interruptions, and disturb the flow in a non-productive way (Arlin, 1979).

e) The unpredictability of classroom life has to be recognized and accepted as well as managed. Teachers are sometimes very effective at conveying the message that unpredictability is to some extent inevitable, which in turn may help pupils recognize this. The skills of turning one's attention away from an interruption, or of learning from unpredicted happenings can be built in the classroom. When it is not recognized or reaches levels for which class members are unprepared, it can be associated with difficult behaviour. Here, the purposes and routines of the classroom might need to be reviewed and re-established for this particular classroom. The process of establishment is usually thought of at the beginning of the school year (Emmer, Evertson and Anderson, 1980), and the process is very illuminating at that time (Ball, 1980; Beynon, 1985), but it may need to be reviewed at other times, especially if patterns of difficulty have arisen.

 Are there any of these preventive aspects you wish to enhance in the particular classroom you have selected where difficulties arise?

Can you observe a colleague in their handling of these aspects in the same classroom?

I *Analysing particular classroom activities*

If you have identified that a classroom difficulty relates to particular activities, the next step is to identify whether there is something about the way we construct the activities which might be improved. The basic ingredients of a classroom activity are shown in Figure 3.2. Scan the

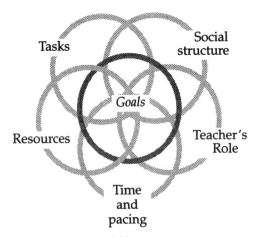

Tasks

Social
structure

Goals

Resources

Teacher's
Role

Time
and
pacing

Figure 3.2   Ingredients in classroom activities

following examples, and see whether you agree that much of a classroom might be portrayed through a focus on features of the activity and situation:

- Brian the drama teacher has a large open space for his room. He arranges chairs in pairs throughout the room and sets the class off on their warm-up task, selling an idea to each other for two minutes while he keeps time. Pupils bring the resource of their out-of-school knowledge. Then groups of four are formed to develop the script for a fantasy advert. Brian uses tight timing for the first half of the lesson, viewing himself as task facilitator and monitor, regularly reminding the groups to use their understanding of influence language.
- Sheila the science teacher has a laboratory with fixed benches and cupboards. Pupils have learned how to use the resources of the room. After a brief introduction with diagrams on the board, they work in small groups to carry out an investigation for about 50 minutes. Pupils occasionally call on Sheila as an extra resource in their problem-solving.
- Andrew teaches languages from the front of a classroom fitted with rows of desks. He uses the blackboard to run a question and answer session for ten minutes: pupils then write the answers into exercise books individually for ten minutes. Andrew sees himself as the sole source of the knowledge which the pupils are gaining.

These brief examples might also remind us that the way in which activities are set up and groups are managed strongly influences the type of control behaviour which the teacher adopts. Bossert (1977) demonstrated consistent patterns in these influences, and the fact that they operated regardless of the individual teacher. Note also how little is said about the goals of the activity in most cases. Yet the element *Goals* is central in keeping the whole activity together and in creating purpose in the classroom. Ames (1992b) and others have noted that very often the goals of classroom activities are not made clear.

 Identify an occasion when a particular classroom activity seemed linked to difficult behaviour. Analyse the activity in terms of the five ingredients and their management.
Make some notes on the aspects of the activity which are highlighted.
• Is the difficulty related to something about the task?
• Is it something about the social structure?
• Is it the timing or pacing of the activity?
And so on.
Now think of a more positive example, an activity with the same pupils which went well. Apply these headings to that example. What aspects of the activity are highlighted as important?

 What suggestions emerge about how to improve the activity where difficulty occurs?
Identify a manageable experiment you will undertake.
Anticipate some of the things which might work against the change you have planned. How will you cope with them?

J Thinking about pupils' roles in subgroups

If a subgroup of pupils seem to be associated with difficult classroom behaviour, we often focus on particular individuals, and attribute things to them – 'ringleaders' and so on. However, the most visible members of a group are not necessarily the sources of power and influence in that group. We need to take seriously the notion of roles in groups, treating role as a cluster of behaviours which is meaningful to others. Role relates to context and does not describe all of a person, but to a set of interactions with the role-partners. A leader cannot be a leader without followers, the bully cannot be a bully without victims.

When analysing the behaviour of pupil groups in a classroom, it follows that we will create a more powerful picture by looking at how the various roles relate and interact in the playing out of the behaviour in that group. Systematic ways of describing roles in groups are not easy to find, and everyday descriptions might not lead us forwards. The work of Bales (1970) has proved useful since it found three important dimensions along which the roles people adopt in groups can be described. The first captured the degree to which the person exercised power or dominance in the group: one's position could be upward or downward on this

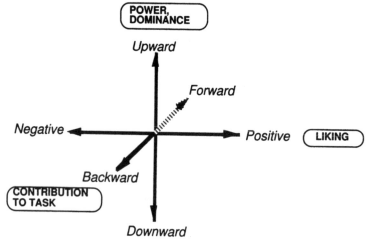

Figure 3.3   Three dimensions along which group roles vary

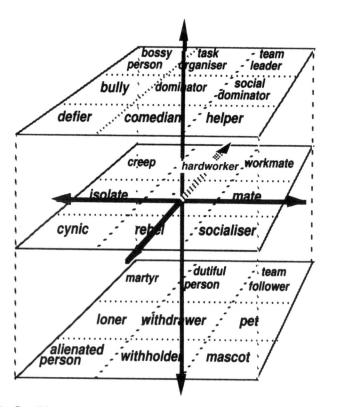

Figure 3.4   Possible group descriptions of role types on three dimensions

dimension. The second illustrates the degree of liking or the evaluation a person attracts: one's position could be positive or negative on this dimension. The third portrays the degree of contribution to the group tasks: a person may be forward or backward on this dimension. Thus, we have a three-dimensional space into which it is possible to locate the general role style of group members (Figure 3.3).

This conceptual framework can be of direct use as it stands. With practice it is soon possible to array the various members of a group in the space by thinking about their positions on the three dimensions in turn. Bales used these dimensions to identify 26 role types, and Figure 3.4 shows our attempt to fit everyday descriptive words to this systematic description. Note that these are not meant to be agreed descriptions: they are the perceptions which members of a particular group might hold about the roles within it.

Applying this to a group of pupils allows us to see the trends and patterns between them. Sometimes we can see that the difficulty highlights a group of dominant people of different styles: the challenge is to harness their dominance towards group goals. Sometimes we can see a pattern of argumentation between roles: on these occasions it is unlikely that one will relinquish dominance, but it may be possible to teach pro-social skills to both parties. Sometimes the role which is being played by third parties is passive towards difficulties, and needs to be enhanced in the interests of a positive group. In the secondary school, we may also be able to collect information which identifies pupils role types in the different groups they are part of for different lessons. The variation in roles displayed can be productive for creating an improved picture in those lessons where difficulty arises.

 Can you apply these frameworks to a group of pupils associated with difficult behaviour? What new insights emerge?
Can you compare your thoughts with those of any other colleagues who know this group?

K *Reviewing classroom curriculum*

Some approaches to difficult classroom behaviour do not include any consideration of the curriculum. This is potentially counterproductive. Classroom management is not an end in itself, and our goal is not to have well-managed intellectually sterile settings. What is available for learning in the classroom is a crucial element in the patterns of behaviour which develop there.

When we feel that a class's difficult behaviour is related to them being 'switched off' from the curriculum offer, we have to be proactive in turning that picture around. In these days of National Curricula and

Think through the headings and enquiries below. See whether any ideas for development emerge.

The assessed curriculum

- Has the purpose of each element of the curriculum been conveyed, so that pupils feel they achieve something valuable?
- Has the level of difficulty been reviewed so that pupils feel the work is not too easy or too difficult?
- Has the work been related to the personal experience of pupils and people they know, and to examples in local life?

The interpersonal curriculum

- Is the way that pupils co-operate and work together a topic for structured review and discussion?
- Are suggestions for improving classroom relations made, both by teacher and pupils?
- Are communication skills, including the constructive communication of emotions, supported and developed in this class?

The personal curriculum

- Does the curriculum offer each pupil the chance to feel more competent at something?
- Has the purpose of the curriculum been linked to pupils' views of their futures?

government-specified initiatives, it is easy for any teacher to feel that they have little control over the curriculum in their classroom. But that is to confuse the broad content with the important lived learning relationships which day by day permeate your classroom(s). A proportion of the classroom curriculum relates to the National Curriculum, but only to your own interpretation of how to offer it, and there is a lot more to the classroom curriculum than that.

We can identify three strands, each with aspects that are planned and aspects that are responsive to the events which arise. When disaffection seems general in a class, the questions under the three headings below might generate a focus for work to increase engagement.

What approaches have your colleagues used to make their classroom curriculum engaging for this group or a similar group of pupils?

L Looking at the profile of activities and engagement

Sometimes disaffection in a class is related to the profile of activities which may have become narrow or repetitive. Here we need to consider the overall profile of activities in a classroom, and their success in creating pupil engagement and learning.

Perhaps a practitioner's list such as this would help to think about the range of possibilities:

- answering teachers' questions (spoken)
- class discussions
- copying
- dictation
- group work
- individual help and guidance
- listening to teacher speaking
- practical work
- reading
- reporting to the rest of the group
- research
- role-play simulations
- taking notes
- talking to other pupils
- watching demonstrations
- watching videos
- working in pairs
- writing answers to questions from a book/the board.

Hughes (1997) collected pupils' perceptions of the frequency of these activities, as well as their perceptions of how effective each was in developing learning. The results shown in Figure 3.5 have some similarity with the findings of Cooper and McIntyre's (1993) studies of teachers' and pupils' perceptions of effective classroom learning. These showed that pupils and teachers prioritise active approaches such as group/pair work, drama/role-play, story-telling and drawing. Nevertheless, the reality in many classrooms is that the frequent activities are those where pupils are passive.

 Might a similar pattern apply in the classroom you are considering? How can you develop a more active, social and learning-oriented profile?

Research on the characteristics which lead to engaging classrooms has been summarized under headings with the acronym TARGET (see Ames 1992a):

Tasks
- Engage personal interest, variety and challenge.
- Help pupils establish short-term goals, so that they view their class-work as manageable, and can see progress.

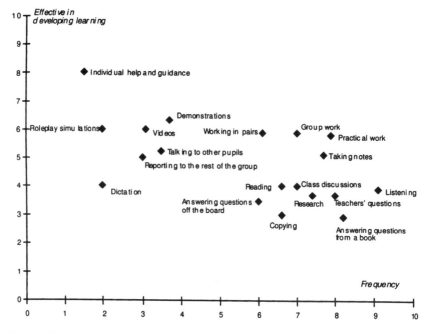

Figure 3.5 Pupils' perceptions of frequency of classroom activities and their effectiveness in developing learning

Authority

- Help pupils participate actively in the learning process via choices and decision-making.
- Help them develop and use strategies to plan, organize and monitor their work.

Recognition

- Recognize individual pupil effort, accomplishments and improvement, and give all pupils opportunities to receive reward and recognition.
- Give recognition and rewards privately so that the value is not derived at the expense of others.

Grouping

- Promote and support co-operative group learning and the skills in peer interaction.
- Use mixed and varied grouping arrangements, helping pupils learn from the experience in different groupings.

Evaluation

- Evaluate pupils for individual progress and improvement: offer feedback and opportunities to improve their performance.
- Vary the method of evaluation and make evaluation private.

Time
- Adjust task or time requirements for pupils who have difficulty completing their work.
- Allow pupils opportunities to plan their timetable, and progress at an optimal rate.

 Are any improvements to the profile of activities indicated in order to achieve greater engagement?

M Reviewing classroom responsibilities

Sometimes poor behaviour in a classroom is associated with a lack of development in the range of pupil roles. Rather than being engaged in creating a productive climate, pupils can slip back into anonymity, and experiment with other forms of behaviour.

When teachers are thinking about developing the range of roles for pupils, they might think about allocating responsibilities for classroom duties. This is fine as far as it goes, but may be available to only a few and may feel trivial to some. So we should consider responsibility and a range of roles in wider aspects of classroom life. Well-structured work in groups is a potent medium for pupils to learn about roles in working together. Direct work of this sort builds from the allocation of functional roles in the group – reporter, timekeeper, arbiter etc. Extending from these skills, there needs to be a focus on roles for learning. This often develops from a structured review of how the role felt, what responsibilities emerged and how others in the group viewed the role.

The most crucial responsibility a pupil takes is responsibility for their learning. This again will not necessarily develop without structured support at first. Giving pupils opportunity to plan their learning activities and to review their learning through a range of appropriate methods is the key to them seeing themselves as active agents in a cycle of learning. For this to happen, it will be necessary for us to:

- clarify the overall curriculum and its goals in pupil-friendly ways
- make plain the tasks and how the assessment will work
- arrange for resources to be accessible
- support pupils' planning and organization skills, together with monitoring and review.

 Think about one of the classes you manage. How does the present profile of responsibilities look under these headings:

- classroom duties
- roles in groups
- responsibility for learning.

Can this profile be enhanced? What would pupils suggest?

N   *Classroom rules and routines*

Rules in classrooms are not operative just because the teacher says so. They have to be set up, agreed, used and periodically re-examined. This is not a once-and-for-all process. Routines also make a contribution: they may not be framed as a 'rule', but they are the way of making regular events happen: how resources are accessed, how homework is handed in, how the classroom is entered and so on. The purpose of any rule or routine needs to be clarified in the way it is framed and through review with the class. If the operation of these becomes erratic then the momentum of the classroom can be at risk. On such occasions, it can be useful to review the steps which are needed for effectiveness:

1 *Establishing* – needs a lot of communication/teaching at the early stage.
2 *Agreeing* – pupils are likely to agree if rules are few in number and their purpose is clear.
3 *Using* – all parties need to publicize and refer to the rules, and mediate them in so doing.
4 *Reviewing* – periodically the class examines whether the rules in use are fulfilling their purpose.

Most classroom rules can be grouped under these five headings (Hargreaves, Hestor and Mellor, 1975):

• talk
• movement
• time
• teacher–pupil relationships
• pupil–pupil relationships.

Negotiation of classroom rules is something which cannot be avoided, indeed Rogers (1991) focuses on this as a major strategy in maintaining effective classrooms. If teachers act as though it was their role to impose a rule system, pupils will spend some of their time testing it out, especially self-respecting adolescents. If more is negotiated from the start, pupils will be more involved in applying it and are likely to learn more about themselves and behaviour in the process.

The level of detail at which rules are phrased can be a trap: if they become too detailed, it is possible to end up with too many and some of them will be easy targets. Once, when working abroad, we remember being presented with a six-page list of rules which newcomers to primary school were given!

O   Discussing the climate

'Climate' can seem like a broad, even nebulous, word, but it is necessary and appropriate for the more general level of considerations which we have now reached regarding difficult behaviour in classrooms. Ever since the studies of Lewin, Lippitt and White (1939) we have known that the teacher's style of running a group has a major effect on young people's behaviour. Classrooms which are run on *laissez-faire* lines are linked to more aggression between pupils – as are those run on authoritarian lines, but in the latter case the evidence may only become clear when the leader leaves the room. Developing a democratic climate is the productive approach.

Classroom climate can be led by the teacher, but you cannot be a leader without followers, so pupils will need to be engaged and supported in a variety of ways as mentioned in preceding sections. Fraser (1989) has reviewed many studies of the social climate of classrooms: his work highlights two recurring aspects: affiliation (pupils' sense of wanting to join in and be a part) and cohesiveness (pupils' sense of wanting to work with each other). These combine with the purposes of the classroom to create a productive climate for learning.

 If climate can be identified by comments of the style 'it's the way we do things around here', what would be said about the way we do things in the class you are considering?

P   Building classroom community

Building classroom community helps to achieve many of the wider and important goals of school. When classes meet periodically to discuss issues of general concern, work collaboratively with the teacher to develop solutions to discipline problems and the teachers help students to think about the importance of community values, pupils develop more pro-social values, helping, conflict resolution skill and motivation to help others learn (Schaps and Solomon, 1990). Kohn (1996) has argued that classroom community-building is the necessary antidote to those methods which seem designed to produce compliance. As for community-building at the school level (discussed in Chapter 2), and in parallel with the above consideration of classroom climate, the central themes which compose community recur: membership, purposefulness and coherence. The link to improved behaviour occurs because students who experience their classroom as a community attempt to abide by its norms and values (Solomon *et al.*, 1996).

Community in a classroom is built slowly but surely through:

- paying attention to how pupils affiliate to the class: do newcomers get included effectively? Do class members feel comfortable to describe the class positively?
- challenging pupils to become engaged in the class, and to support the activities related to it
- encouraging a wide variety of roles and contacts between all members of the class.

When teachers emphasize pro-social values, elicit student ideas, and encourage co-operation, there is higher student engagement and positive behaviour (Solomon *et al.*, 1997). Teachers' encouragement of co-operative activities appears to be particularly important.

Some of the additional methods which may contribute to this development include:

- class meetings, perhaps using a range of methodologies, to plan new tasks and arrange events for the class
- class reviews, which specifically address how the community feels and what would improve its working
- class problem-solving which addresses issues which arise, and through its workings creates more effective solutions at the same time as building self-discipline.

For the teacher responding to difficult behaviour, this means a shift from 'What will I do as a result of this incident?' to 'How are we all going to solve this problem?' and conveying that acts (not actors) are unacceptable when they break a community agreement or damage the community and its goals. Development of a classroom community also needs the pupils to learn skills of listening, anger control, seeing other's point of view and solving problems collaboratively. Teachers need to display these skills.

An underlying theme to these methods is that of regularly asking 'What sort of classroom do we want?' and following through with the responsibilities which we take on in order to achieve the things we want. The teacher can feel challenged at times by really taking on class ideas which she or he may not have chosen. The teacher will also have to challenge any community outcomes which are not genuine solutions, for example false compromises or subtle bargains.

 Classroom community is built in small steps. Which will you take first?

The image of classrooms which we hope to convey

The themes and issues raised in the foregoing sections have not tried to advance a nostalgic, seductive picture of classrooms in which teachers had unquestioned authority and pupils were happily compliant. Rather, the overall position is one of trying to manage this complex situation in such a way that it promotes the qualities and skills which pupils will need to develop for their unknown and changing futures – learning skills and pro-social skills. The teacher who manages such a setting knows that they are not 'in control' of this complexity, but in a myriad of ways they are exercising control.

Keeping classrooms healthy: school practices

The previous sections, which make up the bulk of the chapter on improving classroom behaviour, are presented as though they are frameworks for an individual teacher. It is of course possible that such a scenario would be productive, after all teachers do a lot of their own problem-solving without anyone else knowing. However, you may have noticed that the sections occasionally suggested conversations with colleagues. We believe that on most occasions this can be more productive, since an external dialogue with a colleague can develop further than an internal dialogue with oneself. We now consider some of the wider ways through which colleagues in a school might be helped to interact with each other so as to support each other's learning and practice.

We have seen in Chapter 2 how teacher collaboration is an important part of building a professional learning community in school. Even in a context of pressure and constraint a school can and should provide support to teacher motivation and effectiveness in this way. The image of teachers' working life which we should aim for is one where teachers' classroom practice has been de-privatized. No longer should we hear the idea that 'change stops at the classroom door'.

It is clear that a professional learning community is not built on the staff development practices of the recent past, which too often consisted of staff going to one-off off-site courses, and INSET days where little professional learning took place because the agenda came from elsewhere, the teachers were treated as functionaries rather than professionals and the lack of rigour often led to a dissatisfying process of recycling ignorance. Instead, the development of widespread professional learning in a school requires structural support and human and social resources. What might these be? We comment on some school practices which might be episodic (i.e. called on under certain conditions) and some which are more likely to be regular.

Meetings of teachers over a particular class

We have hardly ever met an example where a meeting of teachers discussing the learning and behaviour of a particular class was not productive. It is common in our experience for teachers who have recently experienced such meetings to say they should have more of them: if they did, the contribution to de-privatization of classroom practice would be significant. In the primary school it is likely that the class teacher remains a central figure in any such meeting, and the more peripheral perspectives of others attending could illuminate and enrich that view. In the secondary school the teachers of a particular group (even though the group may disperse somewhat in later years) can have a productive exchange, especially if it is well facilitated and has a structure to ensure information exchange. Some of the guidelines in Chapter 4 on meetings discussing an individual pupil would also apply. In the secondary school, regular meetings of this sort would be helped if the structure of teams focused more on pupil learning (Watkins, 1999).

Paired observation

Perhaps the most powerful form of professional learning is where pairs of colleagues choose to enter into a partnership with the intention of exploring developments in each others' classroom practice. Such partnerships have to be set up with care, and choice is an important aspect. In many schools, any hint of a central scheme allocating an observer, especially if it is tinged with hierarchical messages, will significantly increase the chances of defensiveness.

For paired work to develop, partners need to establish guidelines and agree on their responsibilities to one another and to others who may have an interest or involvement in the work. Time spent clarifying the purpose of the partnership is well spent at an early stage, so that trust can be built. Some practice and experimentation is welcome on the issues of how to choose a focus for an observation, if and how to collect and record information, etc. We have witnessed some pitfalls here, such as agreeing an oversafe focus in a collusive fashion, or the observer pressing their own interests or agenda as a focus, thereby risking the quality of learning relationship from the start.

The quality of observation is probably subservient to the quality of review which takes place following observation. Here the richness of professional conversation can be very significant – under the right conditions. These are likely to include that the observer will be explicit about the relativity of her or his observations, not casting them as more 'objective' than the teacher's, and that both will join in a dialogue which is triggered from the observations, and which elicits both parties' images and hopes for the classroom.

We are used to hearing that many teachers are resistant to observation of their classroom, and we understand such comments as reflecting past histories of isolation and current hostile perceptions in inspection. But these are not the only conditions under which observation might take place. Little (1988, p. 90) puts it well from her studies: 'Teachers welcome observation and profit from qualified observers, who will not waste the teacher's time, who will not insult the teacher's intelligence, and who will work as hard to understand classroom events as the teachers do to conduct them.' We find most UK teachers agree with this remark and can enter more actively into well-designed co-working as a result.

The following principles, devised from the work of Argyris (1993), have been well received:

- Negotiate your role explicitly, taking care over the evaluative dimension.
- Ask the teacher what they want you to report on and discuss.
- If you ask questions, give your rationale for asking.
- Do not make judgements without clarifying their basis, in detail.
- Beware handling the discussion as a control or influence interaction.

Change is not a problem in an atmosphere where it is recognized that change is continually part of a teacher's professionalism. But if one person takes it upon themselves to think that their job is to get their colleague to change, then the work suffers. Professionally supported teachers move their practice on in a variety of ways. In the current climate of target-mania in education, one conventional message is that action plans must be made for change to take place. We do not find this necessary in many cases, especially in schools where good levels of trust and professional practice are prevalent.

One of the key tests of this paired work, and of the learning climate of the school, is whether colleagues take or make opportunities to share the learning more widely, for example, between partnerships or with wider audiences. If few do, it may reflect on the school culture and, conversely, any pairs who do share more widely deserve real support for their contribution to change.

Mentoring

Mentoring seems to be promoted as a panacea, not always with sufficient attention to goals and processes (Watkins, 1997). Where mentoring is for teachers and has a focus on classroom practice, the mentoring schemes for beginner teachers and for the induction of newly qualified teachers often show the hallmarks of bad practice: agendas are decided elsewhere, mentors talk too much, criticism is confused with feedback, choice and power are not considered openly. The challenge is to find ways of building the learning agenda, building in choice, keeping the relationship under review and supporting action learning at all times (Watkins and Whalley, 1993).

Mentoring pairs who reach the stage of real dialogue (Dixon, 1998) often report a real excitement with their learning and practice. While we know of no direct evidence linking effective mentoring with lesser classroom difficulties, we would confidently expect that a school with quality mentoring on a widespread basis would be showing more signs of a learning community, and these are characterized by reduced difficulty.

Some associated considerations regarding consultation relationships within and beyond the school will be found in Chapter 5.

At this point we reflect back over the chapter on improving classrooms, and consider a further way of keeping classrooms healthy. We wish to emphasize that although this chapter was constructed with the perspective of teachers in mind, and that most of the proposals indicate some action on the teacher's part, a theme runs through them all which is crucial to improving classroom life: improving the quality of communication between teachers and pupils. When difficulty arises in the classroom we may think that things are worse than they are, or that pupils are antagonistic to our goals, and so on. These are thoughts which usually indicate a limitation to communication between us and our pupils. Various studies show us that the picture may not be as we feel it is in those moments. For example, Munn, Johnstone and Holligan (1990) elicited the comments of 543 secondary pupils about the strategies used by their teachers which got the class to work well. The 4,300 comments were grouped into 21 categories, none of which dominated, but the most frequent was 'explains and helps'. A wide variety of strategies was seen as effective by the pupils, and through asking each pupil to select three teachers and their effective strategies, over 75 per cent of the staff in the four schools were identified as being best at getting the class to work well. Staff found this 'an immensely encouraging finding'.

Similarly when it comes to interventions which seek to improve behaviour, the process of eliciting pupil views has been identified in various sections of the chapter and can have long-lasting impact. Swinson (1990) adopted an approach which demonstrated this with a class in the second year of a Liverpool comprehensive, whom their teachers described as 'disruptive, disobedient, and therefore difficult to teach' (Swinson, 1990, p. 82). An early step was to gather their views on their classes, and to find that pupils rated 'being allowed to take a greater part in lessons by discussing rather than just writing/copying' (ibid., p. 84) as the most important item. This item was ranked equally highly by those pupils who had been mentioned as particularly disruptive, as those who were not. 'The teachers were generally surprised and encouraged at the very positive response of the class' (ibid., p. 86). A further step was for a meeting of staff to devise proactive strategies for improvement, agreeing that more emphasis should be given to encouraging feedback from the class. The class were supported in developing social and communication skills, and developed mutually supportive check-ups of equipment at the beginning of the day. Improvements in behaviour, attendance and schoolwork were noticeable, and Swinson concludes that a crucial element was the staff change to a more positive attitude as a result of the questionnaire feedback. In this example, better communication helped the improvement attempt get off the ground, and the improvement attempt itself focused on better communication, both between pupils and teachers and between pupils and pupils.

As we turn our focus to individuals and behaviour, perhaps we will find that frameworks to improve communication will again play a constructive role.

4

Individuals and behaviour

At the centre of all our concerns about difficult behaviour in schools lie individuals. We have seen that school and classroom processes provide the crucial context for these concerns and offer effective means for minimizing patterns of difficulty in school. Yet, given the common ways of describing difficult behaviour, the skill which some pupils demonstrate in affecting their context, and the influential life experiences of many individuals, it will doubtless remain the case that some individuals remain highlighted in our considerations.

A compatible approach to individual work is therefore needed as a strand of our strategies to improve school behaviour. Just like the school and classroom strands, it will not be enough on its own. As that influential study by Gottfredson, Gottfredson and Hybl (1993, p.210) concluded, 'it is clear that a combination of these approaches was effective for producing improvements'. It may well be impossible to disentangle the effects of classroom changes and individual work, since our focus will most often be on individuals in classrooms, but our experience suggests that this multi-level approach to improvement is most effective.

This chapter will review the pitfalls and simplifications which abound in this area and develop an alternative which proves usable and effective for our concerns in school.

Understanding individual behaviour

Understanding individual behaviour is a challenging business. Human beings spend much time attempting it yet often turn out to be ineffective, in some now predictable ways. Thousands of novels and a similar number of biographies have described people and their behaviour as though behaviour was an outgrowth of internal qualities such as 'personality' or 'motives' or 'attitudes'. Yet as we noted in Chapter 1, the consistency which our everyday wisdom attributes to individuals is not matched by the research evidence (Ross and Nisbett, 1991).

In the face of this strong cultural trend towards explaining behaviour by reference to internal attributes of the person, it is instructive to reflect on whether we explain our own behaviour in this way. Mostly people refer to the circumstances they are in, which opens up the following important issue.

A fundamental error in attributing the causes of behaviour

We attribute the causes of others' behaviour to some feature of them as individuals: we attribute the causes of our own behaviour to the situation we are in. This fundamental difference has been studied for decades (see, for example, Jones and Nisbett, 1972), yet has hardly found its way into everyday perceptions and understandings. We find that most people can assimilate this idea, especially when asked to think about how they explain their own behaviour to themselves. The strong forces which work against recognizing this idea are also easy to spot: the knowledge base which the actor has of themselves in various situation, the limited range of situations in which the observer sees the actor, the influence of our language, and so on. Nevertheless, we need to recognize that this trend towards attributing the causes of behaviour in this way is a major feature of our culture, and has spawned a major industry which impacts on our lives.

Gergen (1991) identifies the terms which in his experience are commonly used by mental health professionals and a significant sector of the public in making sense of the self. The examples from his experience in the USA include low self-esteem, authoritarian, externally controlled, depressed, stressed, identity crisis, anxious, antisocial personality, seasonal affective disorder, self-alienated, post-traumatic stress disorder. Doubtless UK teachers could offer others from their experience. His point is this:

> Two features of this list are especially noteworthy. First, all these terms have come into common usage only within the present [twentieth] century (several only within the last decade). Second, they are all terms of mental deficit. They discredit the individual, drawing attention to problems, shortcomings, or incapacities. To put it more broadly, the vocabulary of human deficit has undergone enormous expansion within the present century.

(Gergen, 1991, p. 13)

So the trend towards individual thinking may also be associated with a trend towards deficit thinking. Neither of these are helpful when it comes to our concerns about individual behaviour in school, yet both are very common. Notice that we are not making a moral or romantic argument that within-person thinking is wrong or damaging: we are making the pragmatic point that it does not help progress our concerns about behaviour.

The longer-term impact of individual deficit explanations on considerations of school behaviour is worth noting. The tendency to attribute the causes of difficulty to internal qualities of the pupil is often associated with the tendency to call on specialists from other professions. These are often those with a more medical orientation and an individual mode of explanation: even those professions such as educational psychologists, who do not need to adopt such a stance are pressured towards it. Now we are not saying that pupils in school will not benefit from the help of individual case-based professionals in the appropriate circumstances, but we are saying that exaggerated calling on these professionals has a deleterious effect on teachers. It represents an additional disempowering dynamic to those already mentioned in Chapter 1.

Interventions such as individualized forms of therapy or counselling, usually in a one-to-one setting and most commonly carried out by such professionals, can lead teachers into thinking 'John needs help from a counsellor or psychotherapist'. It follows that John would need to be referred outside the school, and the initiative for working for change is thus taken to be out of the hands of the teacher. Such practice leaves the teacher 'waiting to hear about John' and colludes with the notion that the skilled expert is located outside the school. Teachers unintentionally view an individual pupil (such as John in this example) in terms such as 'special', 'different' or 'disturbed' – a person from whom 'treatment' is a necessary step towards 'cure'.

A major step towards an alternative is taken by adopting the principle which was briefly introduced in Chapter 1, B = f(P.S), that is, behaviour is a function of the person and the situation. When it comes to understanding someone else's behaviour we often omit any thinking about the situation, and therefore regress to individual speak. But every human being shows their uniqueness by their particular profile of behaviours, varying across the situations they are in. It applies to each of us, to every colleague and to every pupil. We find that teachers on courses readily accept that this principle applies to them and their different behaviour in workshops, in the bar, at home and so on. Many of them also are prepared to believe that it applies to their course leaders, who probably do not stand up at home with an overhead projector on their kitchen table, trying to advance professional dialogue! On some occasions recently, when asking course members to offer examples which demonstrate the veracity of this principle, the response has been 'everything'. But that does not mean that our everyday language easily incorporates this principle: it remains the case, especially when brief descriptions are the order of the day, that we can be drawn back into within-individual speak.

Behaviour as an act or part of a cycle

The way in which we speak about, or 'package' our behavioural concerns can have a major effect on our attempts at improvement. The language we use and the elements we choose to highlight are crucial. In particular our focus can be of a limited variety, concentrating on an event, or expanding more in order to identify a pattern. For example, 'Dean gets angry and tears up his work' compared with 'When Dean works on number tasks, if he compares his answers with Leon, he gets upset, says that his work is rubbish and tears it up'.

Psychology in the twentieth century was subject to a mid-century interlude called 'behaviourism', in which one of the principles was to isolate small definable acts of behaviour and explain them by recourse to aspects of the immediate environment, especially rewards and punishments. This reductionist perspective, which made no use of the higher level functioning which is the hallmark of human beings, is still evident in some of the approaches which are brought into schools. In some cases it has promoted a conventional wisdom which leads teachers to focus on 'key' events rather than patterns and sequences in behaviour.

One of the most illuminative approaches to identifying patterns in individual behaviour is to identify the recurring cycles in which the behaviour causing concern is just one part. Usually these are cycles of interactions which involve particular people: other pupils, teacher, and so on. We illustrate this point with an example from a family context: 'Leroy', is a player in the cycle of interactions displayed in Figure 4.1. The concern about Leroy was expressed in a particular way: 'Leroy throws tantrums.' By enquiring about the events and interactions which

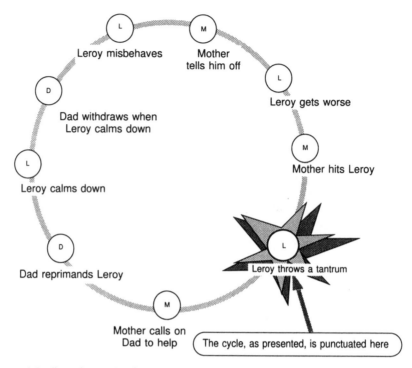

Figure 4.1 'Leroy': a cycle of behaviour and relations

follow the tantrum, and those which precede it, a more complete picture is built up, one which participants can recognize and can see parallels with cycles over longer time periods.

This example also illustrates how the particular shorthand way in which a cycle of interactions is described or punctuated, is only one of many possible for such a cycle. Descriptions may be given which alight on one point in the cycle, or on another point, and the difference will be important. These are different 'punctuations' of the stream of behaviour. A classroom example given by Wubbels, Créton and Holvast (1988, p. 32) has the teacher saying 'because students cause disorder it stands to reason that they learn nothing and get insufficient marks', while the pupils say 'because she cannot explain things properly we get insufficient marks and are not attentive'. The chain of events is punctuated differently by each party. This example also includes a whiff of blame, and of course blame is a very specific punctuation of the cycle with the additional element of one actor being attributed responsibility for the whole picture.

Rather than fall into unhelpful punctuations of a cycle, it is useful to practise laying out the whole cycle, as in the Leroy example above, and to look into the sequence and meaning in a range of ways. This avoids a competition over whose punctuation is 'best', and leads to more creative possibilities and solutions. As we shall see in further examples in this chapter, the practice of identifying both virtuous cycles and vicious cycles can be most productive.

When the picture is not the picture

Most ways of describing difficult behaviour focus only on the difficulty. They often lead to conversations in which no one would believe that there was ever an occasion when the difficulty did not occur. But this is hardly ever the case, so it becomes very important to practise identifying exceptions.

Babatunde and Michael are in their second year of secondary school, and are regularly sent to the year head, John, following disruptive episodes in lessons. These escalate through 'cussing', exchanging personal insults in a gradually escalating manner, leading up to remarks about their respective mothers, at which point a scuffle breaks out. Teachers have tried various approaches: separating them leads to calling out across the classroom, detentions are attended happily and sometimes provide an arena for more cussing. The head of year is almost at a loss to know what to try. One time he asks Babatunde and Michael 'when do you two *not* do this?'. They reply 'most evenings'. John learns that these two spend much of their out-of-school time together, and are in fact quite close, it is just that their style of interacting does not immediately convey this to outsiders.

John's perspective begins to change, and profitably so. He now sees these two as a strong coalition, engaged in personal and predictable exchanges which get them both into new situations – but it is counter-productive. A strategy develops where the coalition is re-cast in more productive ways, rather than appearing to ask them to stop showing that they are friends. Michael and Babatunde are given co-operative tasks to complete in lessons and, if any outbreaks of cussing occur, just one of them is sent to the head of department who finds an alternative place to work. This strategy is clearly linked to the new understanding which has emerged: it values their friendship in its productive aspects, and intervenes only to separate them when things become disruptive.

In this example the key to developing new strategies was to ask about the exceptions to the pattern which so regularly presented itself. This is regularly a key, and represents at an individual level a parallel to the process of appreciative enquiry which was introduced at the school level in Chapter 2. From finding out when things are going productively, we can get an idea for how to do more of it. Identifying the exceptions is a developed method in creative work known as 'solution-focused' (Murphy, 1994; Murphy and Duncan, 1997; Rhodes and Ajmal, 1995).

We have now introduced three key concepts: situations, cycles and exceptions. These form a major part of the frameworks which are offered in the remainder of this chapter. These support a way of working which improves greatly on those alluded to earlier (teachers becoming disempowered by overcalling on 'outside experts' regarding individuals). Our alternative seeks to address difficult behaviour directly (not invoking internal attributes), and to involve the teacher in developing solutions which have impact on classroom behaviour. In this way the teachers, who are part of the situation in which change is desired, are the possible agents of change. Such an alternative engages teachers as skilled practitioners in analysing behaviour, in developing detailed understanding of patterns of behaviour and in working out context-based strategies for improvement.

Ten important questions: situations, exceptions and cycles

In the above sections we have introduced the key concepts in a framework which we and others have used productively for at least a decade. We reproduce it below, using the exact form in which we distribute it. Over the years we have found it reproduced in schools and publications, and see this as further evidence of accessibility and usefulness.

'Ten Important Questions'
WHAT behaviour is causing concern?
   specify clearly, do not merely re-label
IN WHAT SITUATIONS does the behaviour occur?
   In what settings/contexts, with which others?
IN WHAT SITUATIONS does the behaviour NOT occur?
   (this can often be the most illuminating question)
What happens BEFORE the behaviour?
   a precipitating pattern? a build up? a trigger?
What FOLLOWS the behaviour causing concern?
   something which maintains the behaviour?
What SKILLS does the person demonstrate?
   social/communication skills? learning/classroom skills?
What skills does the person apparently NOT demonstrate?
   and how may these be developed?
What view does the person have of their behaviour?
   what does it mean to them?
What view does the person have of themselves?
   and may their behaviour enhance that view?
What view do others have of the person?
   how has this developed? is it self-fulfilling? can it change?
Who is most concerned by this behaviour?

As a first step, we encourage colleagues to try out these 'Ten important questions' by working through an example on their own, in order to see what impact may be made on their own thinking. In order that they do not choose the one most highlighted individual in the whole school (who as we shall discuss later is almost always waving a flag about his or her own abuse), we invite colleagues to choose a pupil whose behaviour puzzles them. Then reading over the questions, thinking about each in turn, they are asked to note what happens, both in terms of any answers thrown up, and in terms of how their thinking is led/influenced. Sometimes they report that a question 'rings a bell' about something in the individual's pattern of behaviour: a new sense is made. On other occasions a colleague will find that they become motivated to find out more about the pattern of behaviour, either by closer observation or by further enquiries. On numerous occasions colleagues report some questions difficult to 'answer', especially those on how the pupil sees herself or himself. This can lead fairly directly to an improvement in orientation towards the pupil, where the teacher chooses to consider more of how the pupil sees herself or himself, and can provide a useful counterweight to simple deficit talk of 'low self-esteem'.

Overall, colleagues regularly report that the use of these questions has a positive effect on their own thinking. It helps to create a more comprehensive picture of the behaviour, and one which teachers say is more balanced or more positive. The development of such a picture is linked to the development of a more reflective stance and a wider range of possibilities for action. The data elicited through the exceptions question is important in that its contribution to the overall picture serves to make teachers' concerns about a pupil's behaviour more balanced and more positive.

As a next step, especially but not solely in the secondary school, we ask colleagues to try out using the 'ten important questions' as a preparation for discussions with colleagues. In pairs, colleagues are asked to identify one pupil whom they both know and whose behaviour concerns or puzzles them. They then go through the 'ten important questions' *on their own*. It is most important that they do this individually before they start exchanging perspectives. Then in pairs, they take turns to communicate their perspective in detail, looking for both similarities and differences in the behaviour they identify, the way they understand it, and the strategies they have tried. They regularly report that hearing another's perspective has helped their own perspective, and that indicators for successful strategies are often developed and exchanged.

In such early experiments with this framework, it is soon the case that somebody spots the flaw in the title (hence the inverted commas 'ten important questions'). Yes there are 11. But question number 11 is of a different type to those which precede it, and it stays as number 11 because its importance sometimes emerges when questions one to ten have not generated any greater illumination. On such occasions it emerges that the person is trying to make sense of a behaviour pattern which they have been told is concerning someone, but from their own perspective they do not have much of a concern. In such examples, question number 11 switches the focus to the person expressing concern, and the pattern which they may be involved in. Examples might include where a particular colleague is expressing concern over the pupil, and that no one else is: in this case a focus on the features of that particular situation is needed. Or perhaps a mother is raising a concern over her child, and the teachers do not honestly share the concern: in this case it can be useful to consider what important things the mother gains through such interactions with school.

Once colleagues have tried out using this structure, they can see its possible use in a range of ways:

1 To order their own thinking. Some keep a paper copy handy, to scan over when trying to understand a behaviour concern.
2 To order discussions with colleagues. Conversations between colleagues can be helped by having the framework in open view in front of them as they talk.
3 To enhance explorations with pupils. The framework may help a pupil see patterns from a more distanced perspective.
4 To improve the school's information-gathering on pupils whose behaviour causes concern. This is explained further in the next section.

One final point is worthwhile. When we first present this framework, someone will often ask why it uses the term 'the person', and does not specifically refer to pupils. The answer is that it may have wider application, both to pupil individuals and, for example, to teacher individuals. The questioner often then tells us that this is what they had in mind. If it is used with respect and with a deeply professional attitude, some of the patterns of behaviour with colleagues may be illuminated.

Diagnostic behaviour questionnaires

Colleagues in many schools identify the potential benefit of collecting views from the range of teachers who meet a pupil whose behaviour causes concern. But the practice often does not realize the benefits. In the secondary school, a 'round robin' may be used, but the structure of what is circulated is often inappropriate, for example asking for open-ended comments on 'behaviour, attitude and homework'. If there is not a more detailed structure and clearer focus, the results may be difficult to use in addressing the behaviour concerns – it risks becoming another case of that old computing phrase: junk in, junk out.

The format which is circulated can be effective if it consists of only one page, containing a limited number of apparently simple questions, so that it does not appear to be asking colleagues to do lots of extra writing, potentially triggering reactions of too little time and too much bureaucracy. An illustrative example for a secondary school is given in Figure 4.2.

Diagnostic Behaviour Questionnaire

From:................................
To: ....
Subject:..............................
Regarding: ....Tutor Group:........................Date: ....
Concern has been expressed about ....'s behaviour in a number of lessons.
The following diagnostic questions are designed to help us get a picture of ....
across all lessons so that we can make some sense of the behaviour overall, and then
work out strategies to bring about change in lessons where there is concern.
Whatever your view of .... I would value your answers.
Thank you for your help.

What does s/he do that causes concern?

What precipitates the behaviour that causes concern?

When does it NOT occur?

Which other pupils are involved, and what are their expectations?

What does s/he seem to gain from behaving this way?

What strategies do you find effective?

Add any other information you feel is relevant

Figure 4.2   Diagnostic Behaviour Questionnaire (secondary school version)

Modifications are possible of course, for example, adding an inquiry about the pupil's strengths, but modifications should be kept within the principles of understanding behaviour which have been suggested in this chapter, not reverting to within-person categories (we once saw a school whose 'round robin' consisted of a list of 43 categories of deficit, ranging from 'low IQ' to 'ADHD', inviting staff to tick those which applied). It is also advisable not to add on major extras such as academic attainments which might possibly cloud the focus and lead to lower quality detail regarding the behaviour: you can be confident that if something about attainment is linked to behaviour difficulty in a particular case, then the information emerging from the process will show it.

The title 'Diagnostic behaviour questionnaire' occasionally seems off-putting to us, but has not been replaced because it is accurate: this framework is diagnostic, it is about behaviour, and a questionnaire. Before long, schools who adopt it use the abbreviation 'DBQ', which seems less daunting.

The introductory paragraph in Figure 4.2 is dense but very important – it contrasts with the many inquiries which colleagues receive in their pigeonholes where the purpose and use is not made clear. The use of the word 'concern' is deliberate, as contrasted with 'problem' or the like. The method of circulation varies from school to school, but a copy in a pigeonhole with a cover note is generally workable. Sometimes colleagues raise questions to clarify the status with regard to 'confidentiality': do pupils get a copy? Or parents? Our answer is generally No: these are the working notes of professional teachers communicating over a concern. Does a copy go in the pupil's file/record? Again No: these are snapshots of a moment in time and do not need a preservation order: they are probably best thrown away after the process which we outline below. That process is the important one: colleagues in schools tell us that in their experience DBQs can be accepted quite quickly because the benefits soon become clear.

The experience of completing a DBQ can be illuminating in itself: colleagues often report that a perspective has emerged as they think, or a new orientation emerges as some elements are difficult to respond to. Some remark that the format has helped them be more reflective and analytic.

The amount that different colleagues choose to write in such a format will always vary greatly between teachers. Some will 'sound off' in the text in a similar way to how they do in the staffroom: this is to be welcomed as it shows the format is not limiting and reminds us that staff feelings about difficult behaviour cannot be ignored. Others will provide a clear and thoughtful account. Sometimes a teacher who is not experiencing difficulty with the pupil in question will give very little detail: this reminds us that the process of improvement will not be achieved as a paper exercise; communication and exploration through a meeting are necessary.

Some examples of the responses which the DBQ elicits, and the process of moving on from there, now follow.

Secondary school example (1)

This example is of a boy in his third year of a London secondary school – we shall call him Paul. Paul was referred to the local child-guidance clinic early in the spring term, by the head of year, for assessment and possible child psychotherapy and/or special education. She was extremely concerned about Paul because of his behaviour, which caused a disruptive effect in school. She thought Paul was probably 'maladjusted', especially since he had previously been expelled from two schools in another authority. She described him then as 'demanding' and 'disruptive', 'clowning' and 'quite physical'. This school, incidentally, was not unused to handling a wide range of pupils, including some whose behaviour was disruptive. In this case, however, the view seemed to be that Paul was 'beyond the pale'.

As part of the investigations into Paul's behaviour the head of year agreed to ask subject teachers to complete a DBQ similar to Figure 4.2. She agreed that as the school was still having to cope with Paul, while waiting for the outcome of his assessment, it was worth doing something – anything – that might help. The particular DBQ used deliberately did not include all the questions in Figure 4.2 since the teachers were reported to be feeling overburdened by Paul already. Teachers were told that the completed forms would be used as the basis of a meeting with all Paul's teachers and that the aim of the meeting would be to work together on reaching some understanding of Paul's behaviour so that strategies could be worked out and then applied in the classroom setting. It was also understood that there would probably be more than one meeting.

The responses from all the completed forms were put on to a single spreadsheet (Table 4.1) for ease of focus at the meeting. Each row shows verbatim what each teacher had written.

Commentary

Reactions on first reading of the spreadsheet in Table 4.1 vary. One senior colleague on reaching the final row was heard to remark: 'Oh, there's always one teacher isn't there!' This is a good way to impose a false uniformity and throw away the key to further exploration. Generally readers need some structure to help them unearth patterns in such an array of information. For example, they might be asked to look at the variation in Paul's behaviour across lessons as shown in Column 1. A next step would be to examine the range of events which seem to precipitate the

Table 4.1 'Paul': diagnostic behaviour questionnaires from eight teachers

Forms of behaviour that cause concern	Precipitators of behaviour	Gains for the pupil from this behaviour	Other pupils' involvement and expectation	Additional information
Mostly – clever replies to adults and peers. Occasionally – physical.	Being asked to do something by the teacher. Being talked to directly by the teacher.	Makes others laugh and gains their respect.	Some other boys expect him (i) to play the fool, i.e. to make them laugh, (ii) to stick up for himself.	He warms very quickly if I show that I appreciate and enjoy his company. I believe he is brighter and sharper than he lets on. There is very little malice attached to his actions in class. There is also very little thought about consequences of his actions but that is by no means unique to him.
Asking pointless questions. Asking for help. Making a noise.	Being left alone. Others are watching and expecting him to misbehave.	Gains admiration of certain members of the class.	Others expect him to say ridiculous things and ask pointless questions. Others will start being disruptive, knowing Paul will join in.	
Swaggers around classroom. Bullies anyone smaller. Swears vociferously and ostentatiously.	Teacher spending time on other pupils.	Gaining an audience. Gaining a reputation for being hard. Creating an atmosphere of anarchy.	A minority get a kick out of the atmosphere of anarchy he creates.	
Loud showing off (not aggressive but very demanding). Laughter. Cracking jokes. Prodding.	Any chances for attention.	Attention – he likes to know he is liked.	He is expected to be the clown by a small group. Peers are always involved: he 'bounced' off them.	

Makes loud comments. Passes remarks to those around him. Produces backchat and comments behind T's back.	Arrives at the lesson already triggered.	Admiration of other peers. Amusement of other peers. Tittering of girls at his more outrageous remarks.	A small group in the class look to him for leadership in being disruptive.	Always appears contrite on a one-to-one basis, although one would be a little more convinced of his serious intentions if he would avoid grinning in a rather inane way.
Works well and co-operates, brings his book to ask questions far more often than most children. On one occasion refused to work, mostly silent, occasional venomous asides to other children.	Only disruptive on one occasion. Triggered by dispute between Paul and another boy about a piece of property.	Considers himself able in German and sets store by his reputation. Loves to occupy the attention of teacher.	Sits alone. Class takes no special notice, though aware he is potentially difficult.	
Raises unrelated issues in P-T and P-P interaction. Will not admit his mistakes.	Work of demanding nature requiring high-level work or long concentration Interaction with other pupils. Inability to accept criticism. Sometimes no obvious reason.	He becomes the centre of attraction. He thereby diverts attention from his work, which is often not of an acceptable standard.	Other pupils involved in conversation with Paul. Some see him as a leader.	
Interested, motivated, most responsive in group.	No disruptive incidents.			

difficult behaviour, as shown in Column 2, seeking connections between these events and the difficult behaviour. The involvement and expectation of other pupils as reported in Column 4 could then be examined for connections with the difficult behaviour.

At this stage of the reading it often becomes meaningful and useful to use the notion of cycles, and to try to identify the elements which make up a 'virtuous cycle' (when behaviour goes well) and contrast them with the elements which make up a 'vicious cycle' (when behaviour does not go well). Let us now return to the narrative about Paul.

In the first meeting of teachers a difficult scenario was created in the opening minutes by a senior member of staff who expressed in a very forceful manner the view that the only possible solution to the problems presented by this pupil was 'to break him'. This view had some support from the form tutor who found Paul impossible to deal with. In spite of this apparently negative start, the meeting proceeded according to the original plan, which was to try to make some sense of Paul's behaviour and to work out possible strategies for change. It became clear from looking through the spreadsheet that there was quite a difference between how Paul behaved in different lessons. Even between the lessons in which there was considerable concern, it seemed that the behaviour which caused concern varied. It seemed that the behaviour that caused concern was set off more by aspects of teacher–pupil interaction, that is, by teacher contact or lack of teacher contact with Paul, than by other factors, such as interactions with specific peers. Given that peers constituted the general audience, this seemed paradoxical, but gradually it became evident that for this young man interaction with the teacher was more significant than with any other(s). No particular identifiable friends or groups of mates formed a consistent audience. It seemed that Paul had developed ways of initiating or extending teacher contact in ways that were extremely successful, but which in most situations created disruptive effects. For Paul, apparently unrewarding interactions with the teacher were preferable to no interactions at all.

As discussion developed, several teachers reported that Paul always arrived early at his lessons. This observation led to the formulation of a strategy that proved successful in spite of, or more probably because of, its simplicity. Paul was to be acknowledged when he arrived for his lesson by addressing him personally but briefly, so that it did not feel like an extra demand on the teachers. Not all the teachers present felt they wanted to do this: the senior teacher and form tutor excluded themselves. One or two teachers decided that in addition to this they would also try to make a point of engaging Paul in brief conversations around the school. The science teacher decided he would give Paul the opportunity of helping him with some of the laboratory preparation on a regular weekly basis as an additional out-of-lesson contact.

When the next meeting of teachers took place about a month later, there had been a marked change in Paul's behaviour. Some felt that something must have happened at home to make such a difference. There was no evidence, however, of any change in Paul's circumstances other than the changes at school, in other words the strategies that had been implemented. A term later the change was maintained and Paul was viewed as a quiet and thoughtful pupil. A year later the change continued.

This example illustrates some key points:

1 The discussion helped the teachers to identify important cycles of inter-action which include a number of elements. The meeting did not revert into looking for simple within-person 'causes' for Paul's behaviour, or relabelling him as 'attention seeking'.
2 The strategy which developed embodied two important principles. The first is to recognize and continue the function which the behaviour serves, but without creating disruptive effects. In Paul's case the engagement with adults was enhanced in ways which were more pro-ductive. The second principle is that of minimum change: only try the minimum intervention which can be applied manageably. This avoids asking too much of the teachers and also avoids the disempowerment which comes from discussing major interventions such as improving the curriculum or reducing the class size.
3 The strategy did not need to be implemented in some uniform way by all participants. A notion of 'consistency' could have undermined the productive outcome by generating unnecessary conflict between the members of the meeting. In many examples such as this, uniformity of approach is not necessary for significant and widespread change to occur. Although it may be tempting to hypothesize an explanation for such change, the reality is that we do not and will not have sufficient evidence. Perhaps small but significant changes from some teachers led Paul to behave differently overall. Perhaps those teachers who said they did not want to join the strategy nevertheless had a different approach to Paul, occasioned by hearing different views on him. Such change reminds us of the multiple interconnectedness of effects in such a situation.

Secondary school example (2)

A similar example now follows because it contains an important differ-ence. In the case of 'Martin', a pupil in his fourth year of an East London secondary school, the DBQ contained two important elements (see Table 4.2) – the enquiries about when the behaviour does *not* occur, and

Table 4.2 'Martin': diagnostic behaviour questionnaires from seven teachers

What behaviour causes concern?	When does this occur?	What apparent rewards?	Others' expectations?	When does it not occur?	Effective strategies?
Never sits still, turns round, upturns desks, swings on chair, makes faces, makes animal and rude noises, swears, runs off.	Usually with [pupil 1] and [pupil 2]. Always becomes involved when there is already trouble. When nothing for him to do.	Impatient, wants instant results.	Not popular with girls, they blame him for disruptions. Most peers consider him an amusement but can become annoyed by his behaviour.	When sitting down and chatting quietly. Sometimes volunteers information, chats and asks questions.	Quiet talk sometimes works. Not very willing to talk about his work in school.
Enters classroom loudly. Gets on with his work well, but invariably ready to join in/ start talking.	Nothing specific.	Popularity.	Expect him to be 'the clown'.	Always has a positive attitude His concentration is better if he is on report.	Lesson by lesson – knowledge of the boundaries he can't cross. Criticism tempered with praise for his work.
Distracts others, turns round and utters exaggerated whispers. Blames others.	Only picks those who can be easily distracted. When teacher stops looking at him.	Completes the work but not to a high standard. Fills the page with writing to avoid argument. When criticized uses this in his defence.	Others expect him to be clown and he obliges. More serious pupils regard him with contempt.	When continually told what to do – then needs teacher attention 'I've been good today Miss'.	Continually watching him. Tiresome and On report. exhausting to. teach.
Talks, never listens, interrupts with	All the time: while teaching at the	Impress friends.	Others try to get him into trouble as he is	Best concentration first thing in	When isolated from rest of class, and from

silly remarks.	blackboard or talking to class. especially in afternoon lessons.		being watched.	the morning. When isolated from the rest of the class can, and wants to do a lot of good work. Positive when alone with teacher.	[pupil 2], [pupil 3], [pupil 4], [pupil 5].
Often forgets his books. Sometimes plays for attention – but not to the extent that he is a problem.	Sometimes easily distracted.	Sometimes lacks concentration. Seeks attention.	Other pupils call him 'shmok'. He handles this very well.	Like most people he works well when he is being successful. Does try hard most of the time.	Acknowledge him and, more important, give him praise.
Does the work mostly – with the occasional diversion into chatter. Nothing worse.	Usually distracted by others.	Attention from peers and from self. Unable to concentrate for long spans.	Expected to play the class buffoon. Although often they tire of this and leave him alone.	Strict supervision, work he is capable to get on with.	Strategies adopted unknown. Likeable and pleasant lad.
Calls out distracting comments. Snatches paper, pens, books off neighbours. Will not return to his place or face the front.	On entry into the room or else erupts at random. Anything and everything is a trigger.	Centre of attention. Lacks a sense of time or place or self-control. He shows a need to please everyone.	Others may initiate mischief or look to him for it – they enjoy seeing him in a pickle.	When conscious of the omnipresence of high authority, in various forms of blackmail, he has occasionally lasted one hour.	Constant referral to authority only partly effective.

the *strategies* which teachers were currently finding effective. In the Paul example above, the discussion elicited these themes, but a specific enquiry at the stage of completing the DBQ can be more helpful.

Commentary

This example illustrates again the fact that behaviour varies markedly across situations. The virtuous and vicious cycles begin to emerge, this time leading the meeting into a discussion of Martin's fooling towards particular audiences being related to those occasions when he feels a failure in the work being requested. In this example, some teachers decided to review the classwork which they were asking of Martin and to review with him the way to get more success in the work. His tutor, who chaired the meeting, organized meetings with Martin over a short series of lunchtimes to discuss strategies of getting on with people at his age, raising the concern that his current strategies were not really leading to friendships.

Primary school example

Katya is an 8-year-old Russian girl in an inner London primary school. Her class teacher, Jane, had already tried out a range of strategies – different groupings, differentiating tasks and involving Katya's mother – but without much change. More detailed diagnostic thinking was needed. Jane completed a DBQ appropriate to the primary school, shown in Table 4.3.

From the account in Table 4.3 you may have started to think about the patterns and sequences in this information, and have developed a range of ideas regarding Katya and what could be done in the class context to make a difference. Jane found that completing the DBQ provided a new focus and started to give her new ideas about what might help. It became clearer to her that the vicious cycle related to Katya not being clear about the classroom task. Katya could be more successful and a virtuous cycle ensued when she was clear about what she had to do, how she should go about it, what equipment she would need, and how to cope with any problems that emerged while she was doing it (such as, not having a green felt-tip pen. This clarity about the task was not so much a problem over language, and Katya having English as a second language but more to do with Katya's skills as a learner: her skills of self-organization, her independence and her problem-solving skills. These were all areas in which she lacked competence and confidence. Jane worked out that if she could help Katya learn how to organize herself and her work in class then a lot of the difficulties in her social relationships and her learning would reduce. A recognition that children

Table 4.3 'Katya': diagnostic behaviour questionnaire from a primary teacher

Current concern	Katya has difficulty getting started with her work: • hits other children in class • snatches equipment in groupwork • does not get on with the other children. She is a 'loner' in the playground, has few friends.
Triggers to the behaviour causing concern	Katya hits other children when she gets frustrated in class. When other children are getting on with the task and she is having difficulty this seems to trigger her to snatch things from them.
With whom?	Katya is more likely to hit or snatch from other girls.
Expectations of others	The girls in the class have been fairly tolerant of her, but some are getting fed up with her and are starting to complain and not want her in their groups. The boys tend to ignore her now. Most of the class now expect her to act this way.
When does she not behave this way?	When the activity is well structured or when it is more mechanical. When she is clear about what she is doing. When she manages to get going at the start she keeps going for longer. When there is an adult present to prompt her through the work. When she does not have to share equipment or resources.
What does she seem to gain?	It is difficult to see what Katya gets out of it. In the short term she gets the felt-tip pen, rubber, or piece of equipment that she wanted, but she inevitably upsets someone and she does not get her work done – it seems to upset her too.
What strategies do you find are helpful?	Things were going from bad to worse with Katya, then we found that she works well in a small group in class with one of the support teachers. The language support teacher has been using a strategy of going through the task with a group and asking *them* to retell to each other *what* they are going to do, *how* they are going to do it and *what* they might do if they hit a problem. They do this *before* they start the task. Katya seems to grasp things better when this happens. Time out does not help, she gets more and more upset. Katya gets very upset when her mother gets to hear about what has happened in school – her mother sometimes gets to hear from other parents.
Any other relevant information	Katya joined the school two terms ago. She is a Russian speaker, although her English is not bad. Her mother is a lone parent. She is anxious to help but may be avoiding us because she is worried about Katya's behaviour in school. She got very upset when one of the parents complained about Katya to her.

were sometimes having to compete for equipment led Jane to reconsider the resources which were available for use in group work. Katya was not as skilled in competing as the other children, and when she failed she would resort to hitting or snatching. So, a first step was to review, for example, whether there were enough felt-tip pens of particular colours, and how any lack could be dealt with. Jane decided to try to give groups the responsibility for the resources provided to them as a group. This, in itself, produced a more co-operative spirit in the group work, which Jane supported further by planning the group work activities to be more collaborative and co-operative. This would give Katya an opportunity to become more of a contributor to group work and begin to reverse the trend of her becoming progressively excluded and ostracized by the others.

In the plan to build up skills of independence and self-organization for the whole class, Jane remembered a strategy that the Language Development Team teacher used: asking children to retell to each other what the task was and how they were going to go about it. She decided to do more of this as a whole-class strategy of which Katya was a part. A spin-off was that children became more likely to ask each other rather than always asking the teacher when they had a difficulty. Another idea the class teacher had was to revisit the intercultural dimensions of her class as a group, and to utilize the range of languages and backgrounds. Many of the children in the class were very interested in Russian and this helped re-establish Katya in the group.

A difference was clear quite quickly for Katya, when the availability of equipment was changed. She responded well to the strategy of explaining and retelling the task. Soon it was possible to provide Katya's mother with more positive accounts. Katya began to look a happier child and to achieve more in school.

Handling a meeting of teachers discussing an individual pupil

The use of the DBQ is to support a collaborative problem-solving meeting aimed at improving behaviour. This mirrors the finding in school improvement more generally that collaborative teams are a key vehicle. Solutions do not come from bureaucratic paper exercises. On occasions where we have seen a year head in a secondary school collect the completed DBQs in order to issue guidance to staff without them meeting, we see their role quickly becoming stuck. They implicitly set themselves up as an expert in interpretation, and they have to convince their colleagues that whatever view they have come up with is worthy of implementation. Role hierarchy may be counterproductive here. By contrast, some of the best practices we have seen minimize hierarchy and maximize collaboration, for example, through meetings being chaired by the pupil's tutor. Of course such practice takes time to become credible in those secondary schools where the tutor role is not afforded credibility, but in primary schools it seems difficult to imagine anyone other than the class teacher guiding the meeting.

The skills and processes of handling such a meeting are worth making clear. Colleagues, and indeed the person who may be running this meeting, may not be sure at first of how best to handle this kind of event. There is plenty of possibility of 'sliding off' into unproductive processes in such a meeting.

The main issues we encourage people to anticipate and practise are:

- Keeping a clear view that the purpose of the meeting is to explore:
    - the variability in the pattern of behaviour across situations
    - possible understandings of the pupil's behaviour
    - strategies for change.
- The key areas are:
    - the situations in which the behaviour which causes concern arises, and those where it does not
    - the involvement and expectations of other pupils, and possible reputation effects
    - the virtuous and vicious cycles in these interactions
    - how to enhance or increase the virtuous cycles.
- Thus it is useful for the convenor of the meeting to prepare for the following:
    - explicitly set a positive and constructive purpose to the meeting
    - keep to the key areas
    - do not expect everyone to express themselves positively
    - expect to encourage some colleagues to participate and contribute
    - keep to (and reiterate) the stated purpose of the meeting
    - do not expect or look for complete consensus
    - develop minimum intervention strategies
    - set a review date.

With practice, productive meetings of this sort can become a regular and supportive feature of the school, and in secondary schools are a reflection of what can be achieved by restructuring in the service of learning (Watkins, 1999).

Addressing wider patterns which emerge from the individual example

By this stage we hope it is clear that many difficulties which arise in relation to the behaviour of individual pupils can be profitably addressed through the methods and principles of this section, without the need to refer to other services. Developing a problem-solving approach which engages colleagues with expertise, both inside and outside the school, builds part of that important sense of efficacy which effective schools and teachers have. The principles and methods of improvement discussed throughout the different levels described in this book have been founded on similar concepts, so from that perspective there should be good potential for interconnectedness between them. It is important that connectedness between the levels is created, since we have said that a focus on individual pupils, or indeed on any one level, is not enough. If someone were to try only to adopt the practices regarding individuals, they would be creating a deeply unethical practice which appeared to locate the causes of difficulty solely with pupils.

Given that many difficulties are reported as to do with individuals, how can we help ourselves see the patterns at other levels, of classroom and organization? How do we ensure that the focus is properly on the pupil on some occasions, but on other occasions, properly on a teacher, or a class, or even the whole organization? Our current answer is through a similar principle to that used in the diagnosing classroom difficulty, Chapter 3, which is to identify the extent of difficulty, in other words how widespread and how located is the pattern of behaviour. If we ask the series of questions at the left-hand side of Figure 4.3, we will be able to move towards the most appropriate focus and level.

In secondary schools this diagram can also set off a useful discussion about the appropriate roles to initiate each action. By asking the staff of a school to add for each box the role title which currently initiates that action, patterns and relations can be discussed. Examples include: where the head of department comes in, which body has the whole-school overview, how the year head role may be protected from dumping with behaviour difficulties, how to ensure an ascendant role for the tutor, the connections with special needs staff (Watkins and Wagner, 1995), and so on.

In primary schools a slightly modified diagram can be drawn, in which the one class teacher and a range of classroom situations are analysed.

When and how knowledge of family is important

The exploration of wider patterns makes our first reference to understandings of family. Some of our colleagues have remarked that we make

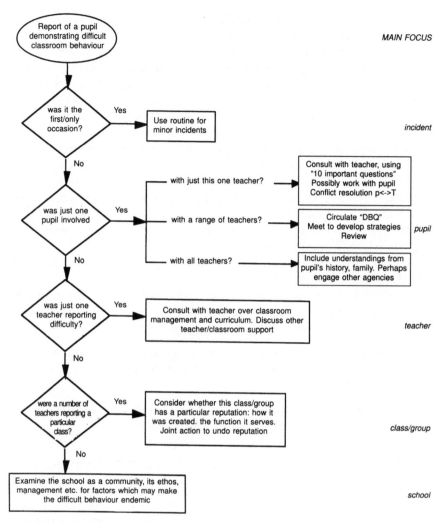

Figure 4.3 Locating wider patterns from individual cases

too little of the family in matters of difficult behaviour, but our perspective is a deliberate one. First, we want our work to redress a tendency often found in schools, that is to swiftly locate the cause for a pupil's difficult behaviour in home background. This is disempowering to teachers. Second we want to be able to specify the features of a behaviour pattern in school which would lead us to engage or seek further knowledge of the family. In this we aim to be more discriminating than that rhetoric which is prevalent currently: that parents are crucial to all school matters. After all, the importance of school is that it is a place for young people to learn about social systems beyond the family.

There is no doubt that the family is a significant and powerful influence on the school-age child, and parental views about school and learning influence those of the child. Schools must work with parents if they are to maximize pupils' potential for success in school. The style of this partnership will vary according to the age and stage of the child, and regular contact with the home is needed to ensure good learning links between school, family and wider community. If schools become encapsulated and defensive, nobody gains.

Given this starting point we hope to assume a generally healthy picture of home–school relations when a parent or parents are engaged to help with the school's difficulty with a pupil. This will maximize the chances of overcoming two common difficulties which lead to poor communication. The first is for the parent to feel anxious and blamed by the school for the concerns. The second is when parents find it difficult to see the school's problem because there is none at home, and resent the school for involving them in what, to them, seems to be the school's failure (Dowling and Osborne, 1994).

So when and how is knowledge of family important? The occasions when knowledge of family is important can be gauged from the results of DBQs, if one or more of the following are found to apply.

1 The pattern of behaviour across situations shows little variability.
2 There is no discernible pay-off for the pupil's behaviour in the immediate situation.

These will now be explored, with examples illustrating how family knowledge was important in improving behaviour.

When the pattern of behaviour shows little variability

While generally pupils are not disruptive in all situations, and behaviour varies as shown in the examples above, there are also exceptional cases where completed DBQs indicate consistent behaviour across a range of lessons. This suggests that the differences between the in-school situations are not acting as powerfully as they generally do. In these circumstances we might turn to explore factors outside the immediate situations. Before immediately assuming a family link, however, it is important to explore all in-school possibilities, for example, whether the pupil might be systematically abused or teased by other pupils between lessons.

Sam is now at secondary school. When she started, teachers quickly developed a view of a rather immature pupil, who was not very popular with other children, apparently preferring the company of staff. At this stage no particular problem in lessons was remarked on. Gradually, however, over the first term a pattern of behaviour emerged which created disruptive effects in the majority of Sam's lessons. One teacher's observations from the DBQ give a flavour of Sam's behaviour in lessons:

- crying
- refusing to work
- falsely accusing others of kicking, punching, throwing things
- hyperventilating until she goes into a panic
- making strange noises when boys walk past her while she backs into the wall.

The consistency of the pattern and the persistence with which Sam presented herself in such an odd and victimized role led to a consideration of factors outside the immediate situations.

Previous school records and a meeting with parents proved invaluable at this time. Sam's parents conveyed the story of Sam as a problem baby, difficult to feed and to comfort. When the time came they were pleased to take advantage of local pre-school provision for children who were viewed as having emotional and behavioural difficulties. For a number of years Sam was attending part-time special educational provision. By junior school age she was attending her local mainstream primary school full time. Her parents were still anxious about how she would progress, so the headteacher of the school arranged regular meetings with them approximately every half-term and reported to them on positive aspects of her work, behaviour and general progress. At this time her behaviour at school was viewed as unproblematic though 'fussy'. The meetings with the head gave the parents a feeling of reassurance over Sam's 'normality' and hence their ability to cope with her.

On Sam's move to secondary school the information about contacts with the parents was overlooked. After half a term teachers noticed the odd behaviours developing. By using DBQs and a meeting, teachers learned that Sam would escalate her 'odd' behaviour if they showed her sympathy and friendliness. Effective strategies were firmness rather than sympathy, ignoring her, and encouraging her to adhere to the standards of behaviour of the group and discouraging behaviour that is different from the group. These classroom-based strategies coupled with a resumption of the regular contact with the parents, providing them with positive reports on work and behaviour, led to a reduction in Sam's extreme behaviours.

Here the school was the appropriate agency to offer a 'normalizing' message, both to Sam and to her parents. One set of strategies without the other would not have had the same long-term effects, because of the particular relationship between the pupil, the family and the school. For Sam, the function of her behaviour in school was to gain concern and contact with adults, replicating the history of interactions in the family. The teachers chose not to replicate this pattern further, and to learn other ways of engaging people. For the parents, their involvement provided reassurance in the face of their anxiety, which was inadvertently contributing toward Sam's view of herself as a problem and resulting in disruptive behaviour. It helped the parents to view Sam more 'normally' and to treat her accordingly.

Sam's behaviour was admittedly somewhat bizarre, but this example was chosen deliberately in order to show the effectiveness of addressing the function of behaviour rather than looking for mental problems or intra-psychic causes. We avoid the trap of making judgements that an individual is 'maladjusted' or 'disturbed' directly from the behaviour presented. If such a line had been pursued by Sam's secondary school teachers, it is possible that they would have mounted a case to label her as needing psychiatric input and/or an emotional and behavioural difficulties (EBD) special school. Sam, however, continued in a mainstream school for the remainder of her school career. The basic question was 'what is the function of the behaviour?', in other words, 'what seems to be achieved by the person who is behaving in this way?' rather than 'how disturbed is the person who behaves like this?'

When there is no discernible pay-off for the behaviour in the immediate situation

The next illustration is of Chris. Chris was nearing the end of his fourth year in a mixed comprehensive school when he became a problem. There was no previous history of disruptive incidents until this time, and no particular difficulties with work. In fact Chris seemed more of an irritation than a disruption. His teachers put it this way:

- 'He does not disrupt but disturbs by not working.'
- 'Shows no interest, lethargic.'
- 'Disruptive is not applicable, he's more like a hibernating bear.'
- 'Not disruptive, but reluctant to take instructions and slow working.'

Chris's lack of engagement was a consistent puzzle, and was not explained by the involvement of other pupils: 'Other pupils not greatly involved but drawn into conversations. They appear to accept his truculence and lack of motivation without imitating it.'

The teachers felt that Chris seemed to gain little from behaving in this way and that no strategy seemed to make any difference. It was also noted that Chris was 'pleasant outside class, speaks first'. It seemed that Chris reserved his withdrawal of co-operation and communication for lesson times and for his subject teachers in those situations.

Talking with Chris started to clarify matters. He saw no point in being in school, and wanted to leave as soon as possible. Meeting with the parents and Chris made the picture even clearer: Chris was going to be 16 years old in the December of his final year of compulsory schooling, and both he and his parents believed that he could leave on his sixteenth birthday: they were convinced that they knew other young people who had done this. Chris had a job waiting for him in the family business and any delay over his starting work was an inconvenience. Teachers had tried to correct Chris's misunderstanding in the past, but Chris had not trusted these explanations and had withdrawn from lessons through passive non-co-operation and psychological truancy. He was supported in this by his parents who, by this time, were angry about negative school reports.

A longer talking through of the regulations and local examples led to a relaxing of the family belief and a discussion of how to make the best use of his remaining time in school. The school was flexible, and adjusted Chris's timetable so that some of his priorities for success could be achieved: arrangements for work experience were added. This led to an improvement in his behaviour in lessons.

In this example, the recourse to the family was needed to make sense of how Chris had developed and maintained this pattern of behaviour in school. The way in which members of the family had maintained each other's beliefs about Chris's leaving had to be addressed with them as a family, before the influence of this belief was loosened on Chris and Chris was able to change.

We do not aim to make any generalizations about 'strategies' from these examples. Each is unique, as are the strategies which proved effective. All illustrate that the way in which parents are involved in helping varies to suit the particular and unique circumstances. The parents' perspective on the problem may be crucial to an understanding of the pupil's behaviour and to its resolution, as in the example of Chris and his parents. On the other hand, the contact may be a way of modifying the parents' view of the child, as in Sam's case.

There are further occasions when a pattern of little variability in school leads our attention to greater problems such as those of child sexual or physical abuse within the family. It is as though on these occasion a pupil is waving a large flag which says to the teachers 'There's something in my life which is much bigger than all these school situations'. Here the school's proper practices and its relations with the specialist social services and police teams will be needed. Occasional examples of little variability across classrooms indicate a within-school phenomenon relating to the spaces between classes: long-standing systematic bullying of an individual may be hidden from the teachers who provide data, and this should be a further hypothesis for the reflective teacher.

Particular patterns of concern relating to individual life experience

Some of the examples in the previous section have highlighted the way in which any pupil's life experiences can be influential in how they are in school, and how their behaviour is sometimes a barometer of those life experiences. It would be remiss not to highlight some of the known patterns in this area, and to indicate what schools might best do.

Recent data on who gets excluded from school has shown some very worrying links with pupils' negative life experiences. Carol Hayden's (1997) studies of primary-age children showed that those excluded were more characterized by:

- family breakdown
- time in care/social work involvement
- multiple moves/disruption
- disability/bereavement
- violence/abuse
- major accident/incident
- no member of household in paid work.

We find that when most teachers are presented with such data they feel keenly the bias and inequity which can be associated with their school systems. Similarly, in secondary schools, the Office for Standards in Education (OFSTED) (1996) report on exclusions found that a disproportionate number of black pupils are excluded (although the OFSTED Press Notice ignored this). In follow-up case studies, by David Moore HMI, 60 per cent of excluded pupils had recently experienced a significant loss or bereavement. Despite their extreme busy-ness and the current pressures to perform, many teachers empathize and review the practice which might lead to exclusion in such cases. Other reactions to this sort of evidence vary from apathy and resignation to angry accusation of schools as damaging organizations.

Our view is that these worrying connections can be addressed and their incidence reduced. This takes three elements:

- that the school as an organization aims to be an inclusive respectful and responsive community for learning
- that the quality of communication between pupils, parents and staff is sufficient for disturbing life experiences to be talked about
- that the school is prepared to work with pupils and support their resilience towards such life experiences and has developed an appropriate preventive and educative role towards matters such as bereavement (Wagner, 1995b) and the refugee experience (Wagner and Lodge, 1994).

The preventive role of schools is clearly within their grasp, and relates to their educative function as a learning community. As Benard (1993) has shown (see also Dugan and Coles, 1989; Rutter 1985b), some children grow up able to cope with life experiences which others find damaging. Such 'resilient' children usually have four attributes:

- social competence
- problem-solving skills
- autonomy
- a sense of purpose and future.

These attributes are exactly those which may be promoted through an effective whole-school approach to personal-social education (Watkins, 1992; 1995), and through the building of a pro-social and caring school community.

For the individual student, their sense of school community is significantly associated with their attitudes, motives, beliefs and behaviour (Battistich *et al.*, 1995). Schools as organizations differ greatly in the extent to which they can be characterized as caring communities for learning, but this characteristic is significantly related to a large number of desirable outcomes for both students and teachers. Teachers and students agree over what makes up this characteristic of their schools, and intervention studies have shown that the sense of school community can be enhanced for both students and teachers. (Battistich *et al.*, 1997). What is more, in schools with the most poverty and disadvantage, some of the strongest positive effects of school community occur (Battistich *et al.*, 1995). Once again, a proactive approach reduces the polarization and increasing inequality in our education system and society.

When we consider some of the behaviours which cause heightened concern, such as drug use and delinquency, schools with higher than average sense-of-community scores had significantly lower rates (Battistich and Hom, 1997). Interventions to build school community are related to significant reductions in these behaviours, and effects are strongest in those schools that implemented the intervention most (Battistich *et al.*, 1996).

Schools that are experienced as communities may enhance students' resiliency, and children growing up in adversity are protected through their families, schools and communities ensuring that:

- there are opportunities for participation
- they have the skills to participate actively
- they are reinforced for their active participation.

This proactive, community approach is reflecting the issues which were raised in Chapter 2, under the consideration of 'how your school behaves'. Once again we see the links between the three levels which have guided this book: organization, classroom and individual. That seems an appropriate point to reach at the end of this chapter, since the linkage between the three levels is important for any improvement in school behaviour and for the long-term maintenance of effective relations regarding behaviour in the school. This latter is the theme of our final chapter.

5

Connections in the school: from referral to consultation

At this point we wish to consider some connections, not so much between the ideas, frameworks and practices in the preceding chapters of this book, but more between the staff of the school who not only want to improve, but also aim to maintain behaviour difficulty at a minimum. If we characterize the evidence and broad approach of this book as supporting a preventive, proactive community-based approach to difficulty, then it may be useful to say more about how the relations between staff work in a school operating on this perspective. At various points in the chapters there have been references to teachers' professional community, school practices to keep classrooms healthy and so on: what do they add up to? How do staff best relate with each other when concerns arise?

One aspect which needs to come under critical scrutiny is the process of 'referral'. At worst this can create a set of relations between staff which amounts to 'pass the parcel'. We will discuss this comment and the evidence which indicates that it is often ineffective before examining the alternative. Here we remember one of the research findings on the characteristics of well-disciplined schools which was mentioned in Chapter 2. Wayson *et al.* (1982) found that teachers in such schools handle all or most of the routine discipline problems themselves.

What is wrong with referral?

In different schools, the extent to which a process of referral is used might fall into any of a number of self-defeating possibilities. The first and most important is that it might not improve the situation. Instead, a regular pattern of transactions between staff, together with the beliefs which seem to support them, keep a self-maintaining process at work, continuing to operate but not solving the real problems. Internal referral systems may be presented as a cooling-off, or as a deterrent or a problem-solving provision. However, on closer inspection other patterns emerge and the exact purposes are less clear. It may well be that the referral systems which some schools operate are a symbolic element of the culture rather than a practical process of improving school behaviour.

We find that the self-maintaining features of referral are easily recognized by most teachers, often by nothing more than presenting them with the diagram in Figure 5.1 and asking 'Have you seen this?' In the primary school the role of head of year in Figure 5.1 may be substituted by the role of deputy head.

Whatever provision exists at the end of a referral system, similar patterns will exist and their self-maintaining dynamics need to be discussed. If the school has a 'withdrawal room' or the like, the conflated purposes and unintended patterns can often be quickly recognized. The first pattern relates to the relations between classroom experience and withdrawal room experience, especially in the pupil's perspective. Stage (1997) carefully devised four different types of in-school referral and compared the results, only to find that varying the detail of the withdrawal experience showed no significant differences. His data suggested that referral was not related to something observably disruptive which the pupil did, such as movement or noise, but was more related to when the teacher disapproved of a pupil's social behaviour. This led him to study the ratio of teacher disapproval to approval in classrooms (generally 3 to 1) and compare it with that in the referral provision (broadly similar). He

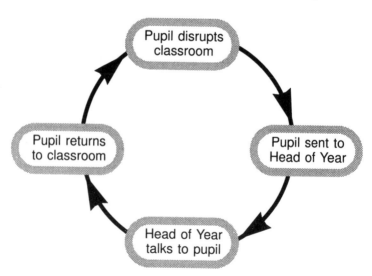

Figure 5.1   The recurring referral cycle

had to relinquish the conventional theory of referral as aversion, and concluded that in classrooms the conditions are created for 'pupil escape behaviour'. In such a scenario the underlying picture of classroom difficulty is probably masked.

An individual example of this pattern is also recognizable. Geoff, in his fourth year of an East London secondary school, was displaying repetitive disruptive behaviour in a number of lessons. Perhaps it was lucky that his pattern was being discussed with the Head of Year and form tutor. When asked what followed the behaviour which caused concern, it became clear that he would find himself having quite long meetings with one of these colleagues. It needed a little pointing out that these two were amongst the most warm and engaging people in the whole school – who would not rather spend time with them? So rather than maintain this pattern it was agreed that if Geoff was disruptive in lessons, he would be sent to work alongside a varied range of senior staff. The behaviour difficulty soon subsided.

Within Stage's data, another pattern emerges, this time focusing more on the teacher. Many teachers, up to 50 per cent at times, do not use the referral process, while some use it a great deal: on average the highest referring teacher accounts for 40 per cent of the referrals. In a larger school in the UK, Badger (1992) also showed the importance of not focusing all the attention on pupils. In his analysis of referrals to a withdrawal room in one year, 11 per cent of referrals were accounted for by five of the pupils – 'no surprise' cry some of the teachers! But 30 per cent of referrals were accounted for by five of the teachers. At this point the challenge is to find a non-blaming way of raising the teacher patterns for discussion, so that the system is not allowed to serve negative purposes for the whole school community, and lead to resentment in staff–student relations.

In an illuminating study, Evans (1999), a head of year in a London comprehensive, examined teachers' use of referral systems, relating the amount that teachers used internal referral to their beliefs about difficult behaviour in classrooms. He showed that the staff who most used internal referral for others to take action were those who believed that they had little role in reducing difficulties. Staff who made zero referrals in three years were either those who were 'recipients' of the referrals, and who presumably had no one to whom they could refer, and those with a strong view of their own role in reducing classroom difficulty. These latter form an important resource for improvement in any school.

We conclude that internal referral as currently practised is an organizational arrangement through which a minority of staff offload responsibility for a smaller minority of pupils – those who have the most difficulty handling the social processes of the classroom.

If a school reviews its referral system, perhaps as part of its work on behaviour at the organizational level, it may decide that revision is needed. Here two elements can be of particular help. First, the patterns in the current system need to be discussed in a reasonably public way, including the possible overuse by a small number of staff whose approach to classroom behaviour would benefit from review. Then collaborative whole-school action is needed to build the motivation to change and to effect such a change: the particular roles which are receiving all the referrals (such as head of year) cannot change the picture alone.

Referral systems often have the effect of reducing staff connectedness, ending up with the different staff in a chain being treated as isolated specialists of some sort. So building the motivation to change such a system requires collaborative work, so that the current pattern can be seen as counterproductive to staff relations. Although as teachers we may feel attached to present systems and initially uninterested to review, this can be overcome by giving voice to the doubts that many teachers have about referral, for example:

- 'I don't get to hear what happened.'
- 'If I do get to hear, people have sometimes decided action I'm unhappy about.'

It can also be useful to explore the fact that the unexamined image of a referral system in many people's minds is like a staircase (Figure 5.2) of which we can ask:

- Is this a staircase or has it become a moving escalator, which itself can escalate things?
- Do some people attempt to take two steps at a time?
- Why are the steps 'up'? Do we think that the colleagues 'up there' have extra skills, or extra knowledge, or extra management responsibilities, or extra 'power'? Is this realistic?

Many schools have told us that they reviewed the process of referral, especially secondary schools which were 'dumping' on their pastoral

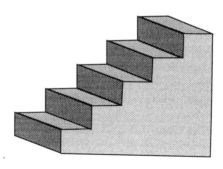

Figure 5.2 The image of referral as staircase

staff, and that new practices have been agreed on paper, but that real practice reverts to the old system. In this process of change the forces which invite reversion to the old system can be strong, because the pattern of behaviour between staff is often not addressed in detail by the paper change. The real change requires new and different interactions between the colleagues. Therefore two action areas are particularly important, as they are the sharp end of creating a new interaction pattern:

- Clarify that if staff try to circumvent the new system and refer to an inappropriate colleague, that colleague is encouraged to send the 'referral' back. Support publicly those colleagues that take such a step. Get them to practise their 'script', and the way they will do this: 'Thank you for coming Wayne, but it is not appropriate that I see you now, so I have to ask you to go back to . . . Will you please take this note to Mr/Ms . . .' In one school in Buckinghamshire, a good indicator that their change was successful came when a form tutor did this to the headteacher.
- Support and train appropriate staff (especially pastoral team leaders) in the skills of saying 'No' without feeling guilty. This should be done alongside the rebuilding of their roles into something more positive. If this element is left out, their behaviour may subtly and unintentionally encourage the old system to remain (especially if they have not yet developed an affiliation to the view of their role as something more proactive).

To remain on the theme of secondary schools for a moment, Galloway (1983) found that in schools which were characterized by low levels of disruptive behaviour, pastoral care was characterized by a principal aim of enhancing educational progress. Other characteristics were that class teachers were not encouraged to pass problems to senior staff, pastoral care was based on tutors from whom advice about pupils was sought, pastoral care for teachers was in evidence and the climate promoted discussion of disruptive behaviour without recrimination.

To conclude, the extent to which internal referral systems remain in school should be minimized and replaced by something better. This will partly be achieved by ensuring that referral systems do not encourage their own use, and partly by putting in place more productive forms of relation between staff. Hence the alternative which we now examine.

School consultation

The term consultation sometimes carries negative connotations amongst teachers, mainly as a result of decades of 'consultation' by government, which showed little evidence of a listening stance. In the professional rather than political sense, consultation is a voluntary, non-supervisory relationship between professionals from different fields, established to aid one in his or her professional functioning (Conoley and Conoley, 1992). So, it is a peer-based relationship where expertise is pooled in order to address a difficulty. It is, therefore, typically unlike the form consultation takes when it is with a medical consultant. Another distinction which is worth making is between consultation and consultancy: the latter is usually referring to time-limited contracted pieces of work from someone outside an organization, whereas consultation is a process that can be embedded in the ongoing relations of an organization and its partnerships. We advocate the term 'peer professional consultation'.

There have been a range of versions of consultation applied in education, and the rationale is broadly similar: the person offering help remains one stage removed from the situation and concern which the person receiving help brings. In that sense it is an 'indirect' service, as the person offering consultation does not intend to work directly with the pupils, whose benefit is the ultimate aim: that is the ongoing role of the consultee, who remains the major change agent since she or he has the most contact time, together with the professional role and responsibility. Consultation aims to create greater efficiency and impact from whoever is offering the helping service by working this way, that is, with the person who has regular contact with and role towards the pupil. The aim is that the skills developed by the consultee are generalized to other contexts and examples in their experience.

Differences between models sometimes emerge under particular labels. Mental health consultation (Caplan, 1970; Figg and Stoker, 1990) may maintain the principles of being consultee centred, but it is likely to focus on individual cases which the consultee brings. It is the 'most psychoanalytic' of the models described by Conoley and Conoley (1992). Its weakness is that it does not address directly the concerns raised by teachers but seeks and explores possible interpretations from a psychodynamic perspective. The experience of mental health consultation often feels alien to teachers and it may fail to develop practical classroom-focused strategies. Behavioural consultation (Kratochwill and Vansomeren, 1985) is likely to utilize behaviourist theory in a technical manner, and as a result its simplifications may not pick up wider levels of the system (Douglas, 1982; Martens and Witt, 1988). Process consultation (Schein, 1988; Schmuck, 1995) is likely to focus on the interpersonal and management processes between staff, in teams working for curriculum change, staff development, and organizational development. It does not aim to address classroom concerns directly.

A model which is more appropriate to the school as a system is a systemic and multi-level model of consultation (Wagner, 1995a). This model of consultation is designed to help teachers address a significant range of classroom- and school-based concerns, using situational, interactionist and systems thinking. It encourages the idea that the teacher who initiates a request for consultation is the person doing direct daily work with the pupils, the person managing the context in which the concern arises, and the person with responsibility for pupil progress. For these reasons they are the person best placed to be doing direct work with the pupils. Similarly it recognizes that the person offering consultation is someone with a perspective on the school, someone with frameworks for understanding individuals, classrooms and school contexts, who has skills in problem exploration. These features place them in an appropriate position for indirect work. Although Wagner's model was developed for educational psychologists, an increasing number of whom are changing from case-based referral to regular consultation relationships with schools, its principles can apply to internal consultation in a school as discussed below.

The focus in consultation may be a teacher's concerns about an individual pupil, a group of pupils, a class, or an organizational matter. As we have seen throughout this book these levels of consideration often connect when the process of thinking recognizes the importance of the context.

For whatever level of focus, the process in a consultation meeting is one which moves through three broad phases of (1) exploration, (2) developing new understandings and (3) action. It is likely that joint exploration of the following areas would be fruitful:

• what the consultee expects from the consultation
• the cause for concern
• when it occurs most
• what it occurs least
• what has been tried
• what has been effective
• what patterns, cycles can be identified
• what the consultee would like to change
• any other relevant information.

A parallel may be seen here with the process of a 'DBQ meeting' with a group of teachers, as described in Chapter 4. A further parallel with that practice may be helpful: before the meeting, ask the consultee to record on paper some of her or his thoughts under the headings above: this process of prior reflection gives the meeting a very productive start.

Consultation relationships: possibilities and difficulties

There are clearly a range of possibilities for who is consulting with whom. For the internal relationships of a school it is most important to consider a wide range of examples where teachers are consulting with each other, throughout the organization. Primarily we imagine peer consultations between pairs of teachers, with as many of the staff as possible engaged in such pairing. Considerations of credibility and trust are central to whether one teacher learns from another in this way: consequently how peer consultants are chosen is critical to the success of building a widespread scheme in a school. In the secondary school this means that pairings will not necessarily be confined within subject departments: we regularly meet colleagues who learn in wider-than-subject relationships and these are a contribution to the community building. In some schools, one colleague may be chosen as a consultant, perhaps as a result of a fortunate combination of her or his credibility, interest in consultation, specialist knowledge and interpersonal skills. An example might be the special educational needs co-ordinator (SENCO) of a school, who regularly finds herself or himself being chosen for consultation about learning difficulties in the classroom, or a year head who has developed expertise in understanding bereavement.

In recent years some attention has been given to the development of teams who operate at a stage before referral to the formal special educational needs process. These may be termed pre-referral teams, teacher support teams or the like. It remains an open question as to whether such a team setting might provide the sort of consultation which we envisage. Friend and Cook (1997), suggest that such teams are still in search of an identity, and it remains unclear how the general knowledge base about teams as professional work groups is applied in the case of problem-solving teams or special education teams. Meyers *et al.* (1996) describe the typical procedures and the collaborative problem-solving processes used by the pre-referral intervention teams in eight urban schools. Some of the findings about team functioning included that the problem-solving stages and the involvement of classroom teachers was inconsistent, and that staff views varied widely regarding the preventive potential of such work. It seems important, therefore, that the purpose, personnel and process of any such teamwork has regular review and clarification in order to achieve productive and realistic goals. Whether such a team context could offer an individual teacher a consultative experience remains to be seen. For an individual to consult with a group could clearly be a daunting experience. Also, the group might develop dynamics which take it in a direction other than consulting. This possibility came to us when considering the views of writers such as Kilgore and Rubin (1995) who analyse why collaboration fails, but in a way that seems to imply that the consulting teacher was a failure for not agreeing with the advice given by 'the collaborative team'. This indicates how easy it is for any appointed team to convince itself of the rectitude of its advice (as well as the appropriacy of its role in giving advice).

These points remind us how difficult it might be to keep to the principles on which such consultation was set up. Perhaps this is no surprise, as many school systems before them have been distorted under the demanding dynamics of behaviour difficulty. This reiterates why the guidance we offer for running DBQ meetings (Chapter 4) is so specific.

The example of DBQ meetings raises the further possibility of group consultation by teachers, in other words, groups of teachers coming together to offer the group consultation. This is some stages on from the early ideas in consultation where an individual professional ventured forth from the clinic to spread their understanding more widely: now we can entertain a consultative spirit being built up in a staff who might sometimes come together to focus on a particular difficulty, but who also might come together to offer a wider form of professional support group (Chisholm *et al.*, 1986).

Finally, an example of a consultation partnership which spans the boundary of the school is important. If the educational psychologist for the school offers a regular whole-school consultative approach to the staff, this can have positive long-term effects. Clearly this will mean that the educational psychologist works on more than individual issues, and in a way which does not revert to within-person explanations. Medway and Nagle (1995) found that successful high school consultation depended on them working collaboratively with staff on classroom, school and community level issues.

Given that we have now outlined a number of possibilities for consultative relationships in a school, the practical aspects need to be considered. Whatever the length of consultation meetings, one of the key issues in having long-term impact is that they are held regularly. The notion that they are only for crises will be very destructive, while on the other hand the distance, reflection and improved style of thinking which comes from regular work will have productive impact. As we said at the end of Chapter 3, when considering school practices for keeping classrooms healthy, provision is best when part of the regular system.

There is no point in fudging the issue of resources, especially time: it is the scarce resource of the schooling system. Professional culture does not develop without time being allocated to the processes which create it. Decisions over time are made differently by different schools, and indicate significant issues in the overall culture. The greater teachers' opportunities for learning, the more their students tend to learn.

The processes in a consultation relationship are fundamental to its success. Collaborative consultation between peers is best handled using open-handed practices and frameworks. There is nothing to be gained from mystifying the consultant's practice, or from possessiveness about what works. The frameworks used can, over time, influence the patterns of thinking which are customarily used in a school. The examples offered in this book, such as 'Ten important questions' (Chapter 4) or 'Diagnosing classroom difficulty' (Chapter 3), contain key elements for developing productive practice between teaching professionals. In their experience Gill and Monsen (1995) concluded that participants in any staff collaborative scheme need a conceptual framework to work in a consultative way, and practical skills in handling their role. Without skills the meetings merely reflected advice, or at worst a reversion to the traditional model of thinking: with the appropriate skills they could manage school-based problems more effectively.

Peer consultation between teachers can effectively link with peer observation of classrooms, especially given Conoley and Conoley's (1982) finding that consultation with observation was more effective than without. Given the publicness of teaching, observation is a sensitive matter and must be handled well, avoiding the common trend of the observer focusing solely on the teacher and adopting a critical stance. As we discussed at the close of Chapter 3, we find that teachers welcome peer professional observation and through it may rebuild trust in their professionalism and learning, distancing it from the hostile witness observations which too often characterize recent approaches to inspection, and which sadly have been incorporated into internal processes of 'monitoring' by some schools.

The evidence on the impact of consultation has mainly been that offered by educational psychologists. In the USA, Gutkin and Curtis's (1990) review indicates the following:

- Student referral rates drop dramatically.
- Pupil gains generalize to others in the same class through increased teacher effectiveness.
- Teachers found problems to be less serious.
- Teachers' problem-solving skills are enhanced.
- Teachers report increased professional skills.
- Teachers' attributions for the causes of problems changed from internal-to-the-child to interactional in nature, recognizing the importance of ecological factors such as classroom, teaching methods and other students.

In the UK, data from those local education authorities which have changed their service model to consultation (Consultation Development Network, 1998) show referrals to full assessment stage of SEN dropping by half, teachers reporting enhanced skill and interactionist thinking, increased work at an organizational level in school, and increased satisfaction by schools. Studies of the introduction of this approach (MacHardy, Carmichael and Proctor, 1997) show that schools quickly prefer it to previous practice.

Evidence on the impact of teachers collaborative consultation is yet to emerge in detail, but there is every reason to assume that it will confirm the positive impact of teacher collaboration and professional culture discussed in Chapter 2.

Principles in problem-solving and principles in school improvement: how they connect

In the 1990s there has been increasing evidence that successful school processes to reduce behaviour difficulties display the following trends:

* internal problem-solving as opposed to external referral
* teamwork as opposed to hierarchy
* classroom focus as opposed to individual focus
* multi-level, multi-causal thinking as opposed to individual intra-psychic thinking, or a behaviourist approach.

The degree of fit between these trends and some of the principles in school improvement which we outlined in Chapter 1 is now great. Real improvement shows an internal process which promotes a cycle of action and learning:

* Check your assumptions.
* Map the difficulties.
* Devise the intervention.
* Review the impact.

As the last word in this text, it only remains for us, your authors, to wish you, the reader, every success in developing improvement strategies at the individual, classroom and school levels, and in experiencing the learning which flows from them, both for teachers and pupils. We recognize the complexity of this work, and also the satisfaction which comes from making a difference in the social world of schools and the lives of young people. The productive connections which you forge between people in school and beyond school make your work a vital contribution to the social world in which we all live.

References

Adams, R. (1991), *Protests by Pupils: Empowerment, Schooling and the State.* London: Falmer.

Admiraal, W. F., Wubbels, T. and Korthagen, F. A. J. (1996), Student teacher behaviour in response to daily hassles in the classroom, *Social Psychology of Education*, 1(1): 25–46.

Ames, C. (1992a), Achievement goals and the classroom motivational climate, in D. H. Schunk and J. L. Meece (eds.), *Student Perceptions in the Classroom.* Hillsdale, NJ: Lawrence Erlbaum.

Ames, C. (1992b), Classrooms: goals, structures, and student motivation, *Journal of Educational Psychology*, 84(3): 261–71.

Anderson, V. and Merrett, F. (1997), The use of correspondence training in improving the in-class behaviour of very troublesome secondary school children, *Educational Psychology*, 17(3): 313–28.

Argyris, C. (1993), *Knowledge for Action.* San Francisco: Jossey-Bass.

Arlin, M. (1979), Teacher transitions can disrupt time flow in classrooms, *American Educational Research Journal*, 16(1): 42–56.

Bach, G. and Wyden, P. (1968), *The Intimate Enemy: How to Fight Fair in Love and Marriage.* New York: William Morrow.

Badger, B. (1992), Changing a disruptive school, in D. Reynolds and P. Cuttance (eds.), *School Effectiveness: Research, Policy and Practice.* London: Cassell.

Bain, A., Houghton, S. and Williams, S. (1991), The effects of a school-wide behaviour management programme on teachers' use of encouragement in the classroom, *Educational Studies*, 17(3): 249–60.

Bales, R. F. (1970), *Personality and Interpersonal Behavior.* New York: Holt, Rinehart & Winston.

Ball, S. J. (1980), Initial encounters in the classroom and the process of establishment, in P. Woods (ed.), *Pupil Strategies: Explorations in the Sociology of the School.* London: Croom Helm.

Battistich, V. and Hom, A. (1997), The relationship between students' sense of their school as a community and their involvement in problem behaviors, *American Journal of Public Health*, 87(12): 1997–2001.

Battistich, V., Schaps, E., Watson, M. and Solomon, D. (1996), Prevention effects of the child development project: early findings from an ongoing multisite demonstration trial', *Journal of Adolescent Research*, 11(1): 12–35.

Battistich, V., Solomon, D., Kim, D.-I., Watson, M. and Schaps, E. (1995),

134

Schools as communities, poverty level of student populations, and students' attitudes, motives and performance: a multilevel analysis, *American Education Research Journal*, 32(3): 627–58.

Battistich, V., Solomon, D., Watson, M. and Schaps, E. (1997), Caring school communities, *Educational Psychologist*, 32(3): 137–51.

Benard, B. (1993), Fostering resiliency in kids, *Educational Leadership*, 51(3): 44–8.

Beynon, J. (1985), *Initial Encounters in the Secondary School*. London: Falmer Press.

Bird, C. (1980), Deviant labelling in school: the pupils' perspective, in P. Woods (ed.), *Pupil Strategies: Explorations in the Sociology of the School*. London: Croom Helm.

Bird, C., Chessum, R., Furlong, J. and Johnson, D. (1980), *Disaffected Pupils*, Uxbridge: Brunel University, Educational Studies Unit.

Blatchford, P. and Sharp, S. (eds.) (1994), *Breaktime and the School: Understanding and Changing Playground Behaviour*. London: Routledge.

Bossert, S. T. (1977), Tasks, group management, and teacher control behaviour: a study of classroom organisation and teacher style, *School Review*, 85(August): 552–65.

Brophy, J. E. and McCaslin, M. (1992), Teachers' reports of how they perceive and cope with problem students, *Elementary School Journal*, 93(1): 3–68.

Brown, J. E. (1986), The use of paradoxical injunction with oppositional behaviour in the classroom, *Psychology in the Schools*, 23(1): 77–81.

Bryk, A. S. and Driscoll, M. E. (1988), *An Empirical Investigation of the School as a Community*. Chicago, IL: University of Chicago School of Education.

Bryk, A. S., Lee, V. E. and Holland, P. B. (1993), *Catholic Schools and the Common Good*. Cambridge, MA: Harvard University Press.

Bryk, A. S., Lee, V. E. and Smith, J. B. (1990), High school organization and its effects on teachers and students: an interpretative summary of the research, in W. H. Clune and J. F. Witte (eds.), *Choice and Control in American Education*, vol. 1. Philadelphia: Falmer Press.

Bullough, R. V. (1991), Exploring personal teaching metaphors in preservice teacher education, *Journal of Teacher Education*, 42(1): 43–51.

Bullough, R. V. and Stokes, D. K. (1994), Analyzing personal teaching metaphors in preservice teacher education as a means for encouraging professional development, *American Educational Research Journal*, 31(1): 197–224.

Cannan, C. (1970), Schools for delinquency, *New Society*, 16(427): 1004.

Caplan, G. (1970), *The Theory and Practice of Mental Health Consultation*. New York: Basic Books.

Chaplain, R. (1996), Pupils under pressure: coping with stress at school, in J. Rudduck, R. Chaplin and D. Wallace (eds.), *School Improvement: What Can Pupils Tell Us?* London: David Fulton.

Chessum, R. (1980), Teacher ideologies and pupil disaffection, in L. Barton, R. Meighan and S. Walker (eds.), *Schooling, Ideology and the Curriculum*. Lewes: Falmer Press.

Chisholm, B., Kearney, D., Knight, H., Little H., Morris, S. and Tweddle, D. (1986), *Preventive Approaches to Disruption: Developing Teaching Skills.* Basingstoke: Macmillan Education.

Clandinin, J. D. (1985), Personal practical knowledge: a study of teachers' classroom images, *Curriculum Inquiry*, 15(4): 361–85.

Clarke, D. D., Parry-Jones, W. L., Gay, B. M. and Smith, C. M. B. (1981), Disruptive incidents in secondary school classrooms: a sequence analysis approach, *Oxford Review of Education*, 7(2): 111–7.

Clarke, S. (1996), The impact of national curriculum statutory testing at Key Stages 1 and 2 on teaching and learning and the curriculum, *British Journal of Curriculum and Assessment*, 6(1): 12–18.

Cohen, B. and Thomas, E. B. (1984), The disciplinary climate of schools, *Journal of Educational Administration*, 22(2): 113–34.

Connelly, M. F. and Clandinin, J. D. (1994), Telling teaching stories, *Teacher Education Quarterly*, 21(1): 145–58.

Conoley, J. C. and Conoley, C. W. (1982), The effects of two conditions of client-centered consultation on student teacher problem descriptions and remedial plans, *Journal of School Psychology*, 20(4): 323–8.

Conoley, J. C. and Conoley, C. W. (1992), *School Consultation: Practice and Training* (2nd edn). Boston: Allyn & Bacon.

Consultation Development Network (1998), *Developing Consultation: LEA Presentation Notes at Workshops 18/9 and 6/11/98*. London: University of London Institute of Education. www.mailbase.ac.uk/lists/epnet/files/consult.rtf

Cooper, P. and McIntyre, D. (1993), Commonality in teachers' and pupils' perceptions of effective classroom learning, *British Journal of Educational Psychology*, 63(3): 381–99.

Cork Examiner (1997), Publication of report on school discipline to Minister of Education, Cork: Cork Examiner, May.

Corrie, L. (1997), The interaction between teachers' knowledge and skills when managing a troublesome classroom behaviour, *Cambridge Journal of Education*, 27(1): 93–105.

Créton, H. A., Wubbels, T. and Hooymayers, H. P. (1989), Escalated disorderly situations in the classroom and the improvement of these situations, *Teaching and Teacher Education*, 5(3): 205–15.

Cromby, J., Sheard, C., Bennet, B., McCorville, R., Richardson, M. and Stewart, D. (1994), Challenging behaviour amongst SLD students: a social constructionist analysis, *British Journal of Special Education*, 21(3): 128–36.

Daines, R. (1981), Withdrawal units and the psychology of problem behaviour, in B. Gillham (ed.), *Problem Behaviour in Secondary Schools*. London: Croom Helm.

Department for Education and Science (1989), *Discipline in Schools: Report of the Committee of Enquiry Chaired by Lord Elton*. London: HMSO.

Dickson, A. (1982), *A Woman In Your Own Right: Assertiveness and You.* London: Quartet Books.

Dixon, N. M. (1998), *Dialogue at Work: Making Talk Developmental for People and Organizations*. London: Lemos & Crane.

Douglas, J. (1982), A 'systems' perspective to behavioural consultation in schools: a personal view, *Bulletin of the British Psychological Society*, 35 (May): 195–7.

Dowling, E. and Osborne, E. (eds.) (1994), *The Family and the School: A Joint Systems Approach to Problems with Children*. London: Routledge.

Doyle, W. (1980), *Classroom Management*. West Lafayette, IN: Kappa Delta Pi.

Doyle, W. (1986a), Academic work, in T. M. Tomlinson and H. J. Walberg (eds.), *Academic Work and Educational Excellence: Raising Student Productivity*. Berkeley, CA: McCutchan.

Doyle, W. (1986b), Classroom organization and management, in M. C. Wittrock (ed.), *Handbook of Research on Teaching*, 3rd edn. New York: Macmillan.

Doyle, W. (1990), Classroom knowledge as a foundation for teaching, *Teachers College Record*, 91(3): 347–60.

Dugan, T. and Coles, R. (eds.) (1989), *The Child in our Times: Studies in the Development of Resiliency*. New York: Brunner-Mazel.

Emmer, E. T. and Aussiker, A. (1989), School and classroom discipline programs: how well do they work?, in O. C. Moles (ed.), *Strategies to Reduce Student Misbehaviour*. Washington, DC: US Department of Education.

Emmer, E. T., Evertson, C. M. and Anderson, L. M. (1980), Effective classroom management at the beginning of the school year, *Elementary School Journal*, 80(5): 219–31.

Emmer, E. T., Evertson, C. M., Sanford, J. P., Clements, B. S. and Worsham, M. E. (1989), *Classroom Management for Secondary Teachers* (2nd edn). Englewood Cliffs, NJ: Prentice-Hall.

Evans, M. (1999), Teachers' attitudes towards disruptive behaviour and their use of internal referral, *Pastoral Care in Education*, 17(4): 29–38.

Ferguson, E. and Houghton, S. (1992), The effects of contingent teacher praise, as specified by Canter assertive discipline program, on childrens' on-task behavior, *Educational Studies*, 18(1): 83–93.

Figg, J. and Stoker, R. (1990), Mental health consultation in education: theory and practice, in C. Aubrey (ed.), *Consultancy in the UK*. London: Falmer Press.

Fraser, B. J. (1989), Twenty years of classroom climate work: progress and prospect, *Journal of Curriculum Studies*, 21(4): 307–27.

Friend, M. and Cook, L. (1997), Student-centered teams in schools: still in search of an identity, *Journal of Educational and Psychological Consultation*, 8(1): 3–20.

Galloway, D. (1983), Disruptive pupils and effective pastoral care, *School Organisation*, 3(3): 245–54.

Galloway, D., Armstrong, D. and Tomlinson, S. (1994), *The Assessment of Special Educational Needs: Whose Problem?* Harlow: Longman.

Galloway, D., Ball, T., Blomfield, D. and Seyd, R. (1982), *Schools and Disruptive Pupils*. London: Longman.

Gannaway, H. (1984), Making sense of school, in M. Hammersley and P.

Woods (eds.), *Life in School: The Sociology of Pupil Culture*. Milton Keynes: Open University Press.

Garner, P. (1992), Involving 'disruptive' students in school discipline structures, *Pastoral Care in Education*, 10(3): 13–19.

Gay, B. M. and Parry-Jones, W. L. (1980), The anatomy of disruption: a preliminary consideration of interaction sequences within disruptive incidents, *Oxford Review of Education*, 6(3): 213–20.

Geiger, K. M. and Turiel, E. (1983), Disruptive school behavior and concepts of social convention in early adolescence, *Journal of Educational Psychology*, 75(5): 677–85.

Gergen, K. J. (1991), *The Saturated Self*. New York: Basic Books.

Gill, D. and Monsen, J. (1995), The staff sharing scheme: a school-based management system for working with challenging child behaviour, *Educational and Child Psychology*, 12(2): 71–80.

Goleman, D. (1996), *Emotional Intelligence: Why it Can Matter More than IQ*. London: Bloomsbury Paperbacks.

Gottfredson, D. C., Gottfredson, G. D. and Hybl, L. G. (1993), Managing adolescent behavior: a multiyear, multischool study, *American Educational Research Journal*, 30(1): 179–215.

Gottfredson, D. C., Gottfredson, G. D. and Skroban, S. (1998), Can prevention work where it is needed most?, *Evaluation Review*, 22(3): 315–40.

Graham, P. and Rutter, M. (1970), Selection of children with psychiatric disorders, in M. Rutter, J. Tizard and K. Whitmore (eds.), *Education, Health and Behaviour*. London: Longman.

Gray, J. and Sime, N. (1989), Findings from the national survey of teachers in England and Wales, in Department for Education and Science (ed.), *Discipline in Schools: Report of the Committee of Enquiry Chaired by Lord Elton*. London: HMSO.

Gray, J., Hopkins, D., Reynolds, D., Wilcox, B., Farrell, S. and Jesson, D. (1999), *Improving Schools: Performance and Potential*. Buckingham: Open University Press.

Gutkin, T. B. and Curtis, M. J. (1990), School-based consultation: theory, techniques and research, in T. B. Gutkin and C. R. Reynolds (ed.), *The Handbook of School Psychology*, 2nd edn. New York: Wiley.

Hammond, S. A. (1996), *The Thin Book of Appreciative Inquiry*. London: BT Press.

Hargreaves, D. H. (1967), *Social Relations in a Secondary School*. London: Routledge & Kegan Paul.

Hargreaves, D. H. (1980), Teachers' knowledge of behaviour problems, in G. Upton and A. Gobell (eds.), *Behaviour Problems in the Comprehensive School*. Cardiff: University College Cardiff Faculty of Education.

Hargreaves, D. H., Hestor, S. and Mellor, F. (1975), *Deviance in Classrooms*. London: Routledge & Kegan Paul.

Hart, P. M., Wearing, A. J. and Conn, M. (1995), Conventional wisdom is a poor predictor of the relationship between discipline policy, student misbehavior and teacher stress, *British Journal of Educational Psychology*, 65(1): 27–48.

Hayden, C. (1997), *Children Excluded from Primary School: Debates, Evidence, Responses.* Buckingham: Open University Press.

Heller, H. (1985), *Helping Schools Change.* Leicester: Centre for the Study of Comprehensive Schools.

HMI (1997), *Inspection Report on The Ridings School, Halifax,* London: Ofsted. http://www.open.gov.uk/ofsted/pdf/3814036.pdf

Houghton, S., Wheldall, K. and Merrett, F. (1988), Classroom behaviour problems which secondary school teachers say they find most troublesome, *British Educational Research Journal,* 14(3): 297–312.

Hughes, M. (1997), *Lessons are For Learning.* Stafford: Network Educational Press.

Humphries, S. (1981), *Hooligans or Rebels? An Oral History of Working Class Childhood and Youth 1889–1939.* Oxford: Blackwell.

Hyman, I. A. and Perone, D. C. (1998), The other side of school violence: educator policies and practices that may contribute to student misbehavior, *Journal of School Psychology,* 36(1): 7–27.

Inner London Education Authority (1984), *Improving Secondary Schools: Research Studies.* London: Inner London Education Authority.

Johnson, B., Oswald, M. and Adey, K. (1993), Discipline in South Australian primary schools, *Educational Studies,* 19(3): 289–305.

Jones, E. E. and Nisbett, R. E. (1972), The actor and the observer: divergent perceptions of the causes of behaviour, in E. E. Jones, D. E. Kanouse, H. H. Kelly, R. E. Nisbett, S. Valins and B. Weiner (eds.), *Attribution: Perceiving the Causes of Behaviour.* Morristown, NJ: General Learning Press.

Jones, K., Quah, M. L. and Charlton, T. (1996), Behaviour which primary and special school teachers in Singapore find most troublesome, *Research in Education,* (55): 62–73.

Jones, K., Wilkin, J. and Charlton, T. (1995), Classroom behaviours which first and middle school teachers in St. Helena find troublesome, *Educational Studies,* 21(2): 139–53.

Jordan, J. (1974), The organisation of perspectives in teacher-pupil relations: an interactionist approach, MEd thesis, University of Manchester.

Katz, N. H. and Lawyer, J. W. (1994), *Preventing and Managing Conflict in Schools.* Thousand Oaks, CA: Corwin Press.

Kilgore, T. L. and Rubin, L. S. (1995), Collaboration for classroom behavior problems. Why it's difficult and how it can be implemented, *Teacher Education and Practice,* 11(1): 28–41.

Kohn, A. (1996), *Beyond Discipline: From Compliance to Community.* Alexandria, VA: Association for Supervision and Curriculum Development.

Kounin, J. S. (1977), *Discipline and Group Management in Classrooms.* (repr. edn). Huntington, NY: Krieger.

Kratochwill, T. and Vansomeren, K. (1985), Barriers to treatment success in behavioral consultation - current limitations and future-directions, *Journal of School Psychology,* 23(3): 225–39.

Kruse, S. D., Louis, K. S. and Bryk, A. S. (1995), An emerging framework for analyzing school-based professional community, in K. S. Louis, S.D. Kruse and Associates (eds.), *Professionalism and Community: Perspectives on Reforming Urban Schools*. Thousand Oaks, CA: Corwin.

Langfeldt, H.-P. (1992), Teachers' perceptions of problem behaviour: a cross-cultural study between Germany and South Korea, *British Journal of Educational Psychology*, 62(2): 217–24.

Lawrence, J., Steed, D. and Young, P. (1977), *Disruptive Behaviour in a Secondary School*. Educational Studies Monograph No. 1. London: University of London Goldsmiths College.

Lawrence, J., Steed, D. and Young, P. (1981), *Dialogue on Disruptive Behaviour*. London: PJD Press.

Lawrence, J., Steed, D. and Young, P. (1989), *Disruptive Pupils – Disruptive schools?* London: Routledge.

Lee, V. E., Bryk, A. S. and Smith, J. B. (1993), The organization of effective secondary schools, *Review of Research in Education*, 19: 171–267.

Lewin, K. (1946), Behavior and development as a function of the total situation, in L. Carmichael (ed.), *Manual of Child Psychology*. New York: Wiley.

Lewin, K., Lippitt, R. and White, R. (1939), Patterns of aggressive behavior in experimentally created social climates, *Journal of Social Psychology*, 10 (May): 271–99.

Little, J. W. (1988), Assessing the prospects for teacher leadership, in A. Lieberman (ed.), *Building a Professional Culture in Schools*. New York: Teachers College Press.

MacHardy, L., Carmichael, H. and Proctor, J. (1997), *School Consultation: An Evaluation Study of a Model of Service Delivery*, Aberdeen: Aberdeen City Council Psychological Service.

Martens, B. K. and Witt, J. C. (1988), Expanding the scope of behavioral consultation: a systems approach to classroom behavior, *Professional School Psychology*, 3: 271–81.

Maxwell, W. S. (1987), Teachers' attitudes towards disruptive behaviour in secondary schools, *Educational Review*, 39(3): 203–16.

Medway, F. J. and Nagle, R. J. (1995), Improving discipline in a high school, in J. L. Alpert (ed.), *Psychological Consultation in Educational Settings: Casebook for Working with Administrators, Teachers, Students and Community*, 2nd edn. Northvale, NJ: Jason Aronson.

Merrett, F. and Taylor, B. (1994), Behaviour problems in the nursery, *Educational Review*, 46(3): 287–95.

Metz, M. H. (1986), *Different by Design: The Context and Character of Three Magnet Schools*. New York: Routledge & Kegan Paul.

Meyers, B., Valentino, C., Meyers, J., Baretti, M. and Brent, D. (1996), Implementing prereferral intervention teams as an approach to school-based consultation in an urban school system, *Journal of Educational and Psychological Consultation*, 7(2): 119–49.

Milgram, S. (1963), Behavioral study of obedience, *Journal of Abnormal and Social Psychology*, 67(4): 271–378.

Milgram, S. (1992), *The Individual in a Social World: Essays and Experiments* (2nd edn.). London: McGraw-Hill.

Miller, A. (1995), Teachers' attributions of causality, control and responsibility in respect of difficult pupil behaviour and its successful management, *Educational Psychology*, 15(4): 457–71.

Minuchin, P. P. and Shapiro, E. K. (1983), The school as a context for social development, in P. H. Mussen (ed.), *Handbook of Child Psychology*, Vol 4: *Socialization, Personality and Social Development*. New York: Wiley.

Minuchin, P. P., Biber, B., Shapiro, E. K. and Zimiles, H. (1969), *The Psychological Impact of School Experience*. New York: Basic Books.

Mortimore, P. (1980), Misbehaviour in schools, in G. Upton and A. Gobell (eds.), *Behaviour Problems in the Comprehensive School*. Cardiff: University College Faculty of Education.

Mortimore, P. and Whitty, G. (1997), *Can School Improvement Overcome the Effects of Disadvantage?* London: Institute of Education.

Mortimore, P., Davies, J., Varlaam, A. and West, A. (1983), *Behaviour Problems in Schools: An Evaluation of Support Centres*. London: Croom Helm.

Munn, P., Johnstone, M. and Holligan, C. (1990), Pupils' perceptions of 'effective disciplinarians', *British Educational Research Journal*, 16(2): 191–8.

Murphy, J. J. (1994), Working with what works: a solution-focused approach to school behavior problems, *School Counselor*, 42(1): 59–65.

Murphy, J. J. and Duncan, B. L. (1997), *Brief Intervention for School Problems: Collaborating for Practical Solutions*. New York: Guilford Press.

National Commission on Education (1996), *Success Against the Odds: Effective Schools in Disadvantaged Areas*. London: Routledge.

Newmann, F. M., Marks, H. M. and Gamoran, A. (1995), Authentic pedagogy and student performance, *American Journal of Education*, 104(4): 280–312.

Nicholls, D. and Houghton, S. (1995), The effect of Canter's assertive discipline program on teacher and student behavior, *British Journal of Educational Psychology*, 65(2): 197–210.

O'Hagan, F. J. and Edmunds, G. (1982), Pupils' attitudes towards teachers' strategies for controlling disruptive behaviour, *British Journal of Educational Psychology*, 52(3): 331–40.

Office for Standards in Education (1996), *Exclusions from Secondary Schools 1995/6: A Report from the Office of Her Majesty's Chief Inspector of Schools*. London: The Stationery Office.

Office for Standards in Education (1998), *Secondary Education 1993-1997: A Review of Secondary Schools in England*. London: The Stationery Office.

Pearson, G. (1983), *Hooligan: A History of Respectable Fears*. New York: Schocken.

Power, M. J., Alderson, M. R., Phillipson, C. M., Schoenberg, E. and Morris, J. M. (1967), Delinquent schools, *New Society*, 10, 19 October: 542–3.

Poyner, B. and Warne, C. (1988), *Preventing Violence to Staff*. London: HMSO/Health and Safety Executive.

Rabinowitz, A. (1981), The range of solutions: a critical analysis, in B. Gillham (ed.), *Problem Behaviour in Secondary Schools*. London: Croom Helm.

Reynolds, D. (1976), When teachers and pupils refuse a truce: the secondary school and the creation of delinquency, in G. Mungham and G. Pearson (eds.), *Working Class Youth Cultures*. London: Routledge & Kegan Paul.

Reynolds, D. and Murgatroyd, S. (1977a), Towards a socio-psychological view of truancy, in B. Kahan (ed.), *Working Together for Children and their Families*. London: HMSO.

Reynolds, D. and Murgatroyd, S. (1977b), The sociology of schooling and the absent pupil: the school as a factor in the generation of truancy, in H. Carroll (ed.), *Absenteeism in South Wales*. Swansea: University College Faculty of Education.

Rhodes, J. and Ajmal, Y. (1995), *Solution Focused Thinking in Schools: Behaviour, Reading and Organisation*. London: BT Press.

Rogers, B. (1991), *'You Know the Fair Rule': Strategies for Making the Hard Job of Discipline in School Easier*. Harlow: Longman.

Rogers, B. (1992), Students who want the last word, *Support for Learning*, 7(4): 166–70.

Roland, E. (1989), A system oriented strategy against bullying, in E. Roland and E. Munthe (eds.), *Bullying: An International Perspective*. London: David Fulton.

Rosenholtz, S. J. (1989), *Teachers' Workplace: The Social Organization of Schools*. New York: Longman.

Ross, L. (1977), The intuitive psychologist and his shortcomings, in L. Berkowitz (ed.), *Advances in Experimental Social Psychology*, Vol. 10. New York: Academic Press.

Ross, L. and Nisbett, R. (1991), *The Person and the Situation: Perspectives of Social Psychology*. London: McGraw-Hill.

Rutter, M. (1985a), Family and school influences on behavioural development, *Journal of Child Psychology and Child Psychiatry*, 26(3): 349–68.

Rutter, M. (1985b), Resilience in the face of adversity: protective factors and resistance to psychiatric disorder, *British Journal of Psychiatry*, 147(6): 598–611.

Rutter, M., Maughan, B., Mortimore, P. and Ouston, J. (1979), *Fifteen Thousand Hours: secondary schools and their effects*. London: Open Books.

Ryans, D. G. (1968), *Characteristics of Teachers: Their Description, Comparison and Approval: A Research Study*. Washington, DC: American Council on Education.

Schaps, E. and Solomon, D. (1990), Schools and classrooms as caring communities, *Educational Leadership*, 48(3): 38–42.

Schein, E. H. (1988), *Process Consultation: Its Role in Organization Development* (2nd edn). Wokingham: Addison-Wesley.

Schmuck, R. (1995), Process consultation and organization-development today, *Journal of Educational and Psychological Consultation*, 6(3): 207–15.

Senge, P. M. (1990), *The Fifth Discipline: The Art and Practice of the Learning Organisation*. London: Century Business.

Sergiovanni, T. J. (1994), *Building Community in Schools*. San Francisco: Jossey-Bass.

Sharp, S. (1996), The role of peers in tackling bullying in schools, *Educational Psychology in Practice*, 11(4): 17–22.

Sharp, S. (1997), *Reducing School Bullying – What Works?*, Coventry: National Association for Pastoral Care in Education.

Sharp, S. and Smith, P. K. (1994), *Tackling Bullying in your School: A Practical Handbook for Teachers*. London: Routledge.

Silverstein, J. M. (1979), Individual and environmental correlates of pupil problematic and non-problematic behavior, Doctorate thesis, New York University.

Smith, P. K. and Sharp, S. (eds.) (1994), *School Bullying: Insights and Perspectives*. London: Routledge.

Solomon, D., Battistich, V., Kim, D.-I. and Watson, M. (1997), Teacher practices associated with students' sense of the classroom as a community, *Social Psychology of Education*, 1(3): 235–67.

Solomon, D., Watson, M., Battistich, V., Schaps, E. and Delucchi, K. (1996), Creating classrooms that students experience as communities, *American Journal of Community Psychology*, 24(6): 719–48.

Stage, S. A. (1997), A preliminary investigation of the relationship between in-school suspension and the disruptive classroom behavior of students with behavioral disorders, *Behavioral Disorders*, 23(1): 57–76.

Steed, D. (1983), Tired of school: Danish disruptive pupils and ours, *Cambridge Journal of Education*, 12(1): 20–5.

Stevens, R. and Slavin, R. (1995), The cooperative elementary school: effects on students' achievement, attitudes, and social relations, *American Educational Research Journal*, 32(2): 321–51.

Stoll, L. A. and Fink, D. (1996), *Changing Our Schools: Linking School Effectiveness and School Improvement*. Buckingham: Open University Press.

Stoll, L. and Myers, K. (eds.) (1998), *No Quick Fixes: Perspectives on Schools in Difficulty*. London: Falmer Press.

Swinson, J. (1990), Improving behaviour: a whole-class approach using pupil perceptions and social skills training, *Educational Psychology in Practice*, 6(2): 82–9.

Sykes, G. and Matza, D. (1957), Techniques for neutralising deviant identity, *American Sociological Review*, 22(6): 667–70.

Tattum, D. P. (1982), *Disruptive Pupils in Schools and Units*. Chichester: Wiley.

Taylor, N. (1993), Ability grouping and its effect on pupil behaviour: a case study of a Midlands comprehensive school, *Education Today*, 43(2): 14–17.

Tomlinson, J. R. G. (1986), Public education, public good, Inaugural lecture, 2 June, Warwick University.

Wagner, P. (1995a), *School Consultation: Frameworks for the Practising Educational Psychologist*. London: Kensington and Chelsea Educational Psychology Service.

Wagner, P. (1995b), Schools and pupils: developing their responses to bereavement, in R. Best, P. Lang, C. Lodge, and C. Watkins (eds.), *Pastoral Care and Personal-Social Education: Entitlement and Provision*. London: Cassell.

Wagner, P. and Lodge, C. (1994), *Refugee Children in School*. Coventry: National Association for Pastoral Care in Education.

Watkins, C. (1992), *Whole School Personal-Social Education: Policy and Practice*.

Coventry: National Association for Pastoral Care in Education.

Watkins, C. (1995), The value of Pastoral Care and PSE, in R. Best, P. Lang, C. Lodge and C. Watkins (eds.), *Pastoral Care and Personal-Social Education: Entitlement and Provision.* London: Cassell.

Watkins, C. (1997), Clarifying mentoring goals in their context, in J. Stephenson (ed.), *Mentoring – the New Panacea?* Dereham: Peter Francis.

Watkins, C. (1998), Trends in exclusion and patterns of provision for excluded pupils, paper presented at British Psychological Society Annual Conference, Brighton.

Watkins, C. (1999), The case for restructuring the UK secondary school, *Pastoral Care in Education,* 17(4): 3–10.

Watkins, C. and Mortimore, P. (1999), Pedagogy: what do we know? in P. Mortimore (ed.), *Pedagogy and its Impact on Learning.* London: Paul Chapman/Sage.

Watkins, C. and Wagner, P. (1995), School Behaviour and Special Educational Needs – what's the link?, in P. Stobbs (ed.), *Schools' SEN Policies Pack: Discussion Papers 1.* London: National Children's Bureau.

Watkins, C. and Whalley, C. (1993), *Mentoring: Resources for School-Based Development.* Harlow: Longman.

Wayson, W. W., deVoss, G. G., Kaeser, S. C., Lasley, T. and Pinnel, G. S. (1982), *Handbook for Developing Schools with Good Discipline.* Bloomington, IN: Phi Delta Kappa.

Weinstein, C. S. (1979), The physical environment of the school: a review of the research, *Review of Educational Research,* 49(4): 577–610.

Weinstein, C. S. (1991), The classroom as a social context for learning, *Annual Review of Psychology,* 42: 493–525.

Welsh, W., Greene, J. and Jenkins, P. (1999), School disorder: the influence of individual, institutional, and community factors, *Criminology,* 37(1): 73–115.

Westheimer, J. and Kahne, J. (1993), Building school communities: an experience-based model, *Phi Delta Kappa,* 75(4): 324–28.

Wheldall, K. and Merrett, F. (1988), Which classroom behaviours do primary school teachers say they find most troublesome?, *Educational Review,* 40(1): 13–27.

Wubbels, T., Créton, H. A. and Holvast, A. (1988), Undesirable classroom situations: a systems communication perspective, *Interchange,* 19(2): 25–40.

Young, P., Steed, D. and Lawrence, J. (1980), Local Education Authority responses to disruptive behaviour: a research note, *Policy and Politics,* 7: 387–93.

Name Index

145

Subject Index

146